The Beat Goes On

Liverpool, Popular Music and the Changing City

EDITED BY

Marion Leonard and Robert Strachan

LIVERPOOL UNIVERSITY PRESS

First published 2010 by
Liverpool University Press
4 Cambridge Street
Liverpool
L69 7ZU

Copyright © 2010 Liverpool University Press

The right of Marion Leonard and Robert Strachan to be identified
as the editors of this work has been asserted by them in accordance
with the Copyright, Designs and Patents Act, 1988.

British Library Cataloguing-in-Publication Data
A British Library CIP Record is available

ISBN   978-1-84631-189-5   *cased*
ISBN   978-1-84631-190-1   *limp*

Typeset in Charter by R. J. Footring Ltd, Derby
Printed and bound in the UK by Bell and Bain Ltd, Glasgow

Wakefield L'
& Inforr
The Beat Goes On

Contents

Contents

List of contributors

Sara Cohen is a Professor in the School of Music and Director of the Institute of Popular Music at the University of Liverpool, and she has a DPhil in social anthropology from Oxford University. While her publications address various aspects of popular music culture she has specialized in ethnographic research on popular music and in the study of music, place and urban environments. She is author of *Rock Culture in Liverpool* (1991) and *Decline, Renewal and the City in Popular Music Culture* (2007).

Ian Inglis is Reader in Popular Music Studies at the University of Northumbria. He has written extensively about the music and career of the Beatles. His books include *The Beatles, Popular Music and Society* (2000); *Popular Music and Film* (2003); *Performance and Popular Music* (2006); *The Words and Music of George Harrison* (2010); *Popular Music and Television in Britain* (2010); and *The Beatles and Hamburg* (2011).

Brett Lashua is a Lecturer in the Carnegie Faculty of Sport and Education at Leeds Metropolitan University. From 2007 to 2009 he was Research Associate at the University of Liverpool's Institute of Popular Music, working on the project 'Popular Musicscapes and the Characterization of the Urban Environment', funded by the Arts and Humanities Research Council. He holds a PhD in leisure studies from the University of Alberta (Canada). His research interests include ethnographic studies of leisure, young people, music making and urban spaces.

Spencer Leigh is a journalist and broadcaster who was born in Liverpool in 1945. He is presenter of the weekly *On the Beat* music show on BBC Radio Merseyside. He writes extensively on popular music, often contributing obituaries to the *Independent*, and has published numerous books, including *Wondrous Face: The Billy Fury Story* (2005), *The Cavern: The Most Famous Club in the World* (2008) and *Everyday: Getting Closer to Buddy Holly* (2009).

Marion Leonard is a Senior Lecturer in the School of Music at the University of Liverpool and member of the University's Institute of Popular Music. Her scholarly output includes works on gender, the music industry, and the collection and display of popular music in museums. Her monograph *Gender in the Music Industry* was published by Ashgate in 2007. From 2006 to 2008, she was seconded to National Museums Liverpool as lead curator for *The Beat Goes On*, an exhibition on popular music which was shown at World Museum Liverpool from July 2008 to November 2009.

Robert Strachan is a Lecturer in the School of Music at the University of Liverpool. He has published scholarly work on DIY music scenes, documentary film, music video, music biography and the music industry. He is commissioning editor of the journal *Popular Music History*, published by Equinox. He holds a PhD in music from the University of Liverpool.

Georgina Young is a social history curator who worked on *The Beat Goes On* exhibition for National Museums Liverpool. She specializes in collecting and interpreting contemporary social and cultural history and has worked for the Museum of Liverpool, Museum of Croydon, Museum of London and Warwickshire Museum, among others. Georgina studied history at the University of Warwick and museology at the University of East Anglia.

List of illustrations

Lita Roza. © Lita Roza.

Bill Harry, founder of *Mersey Beat*. © National Museums Liverpool.

The Chants at the Cavern Club. Courtesy of Joe Ankrah.

The Beatles appearing on *The Ed Sullivan Show* in 1964. © National Museums Liverpool.

Gerry Marsden and Cilla Black. © National Museums Liverpool.

Beryl Marsden with Lee Curtis' All-Stars. Courtesy of the *Liverpool Daily Post and Echo*.

Supercharge at the Sportsman pub, St Johns precinct. Courtesy of Tony Bolland.

Exterior of St Johns precinct, with the Top Rank Suite ballroom in view. Courtesy of Liverpool Record Office, Liverpool Libraries.

The Real Thing. Redferns Music Picture Library.

Eric's flyer, designed by Steve Hardstaff. Courtesy of Norman Killon.

Club regular Mark Jordan and friends outside Eric's, Mathew Street. Courtesy of Mark Jordan.

Acknowledgements

This book is a collection of essays which expands upon the research undertaken for *The Beat Goes On*, an exhibition which opened as part of Liverpool's European Capital of Culture celebrations in 2008. The exhibition by National Museums Liverpool (NML) was researched in conjunction with the Institute of Popular Music at the University of Liverpool. We would like to give thanks for the support and encouragement of NML during the development of the book and we are especially grateful to Janet Dugdale, Jen Cunnington and David Fleming. We must also thank those with responsibility for research and publications at NML for their support, particularly Kay Carson, John Murden and Karen Miller. We would like to express our appreciation of those who worked on the production of the book, especially Anthony Cond, Charly Paige and Helen Tookey at Liverpool University Press, Ralph Footring for his careful production editing and Justina Heslop at NML for image research.

The book would not have been possible without the hard work of those within the Urban History Department at NML. It draws extensively on oral histories undertaken for the project by Paul Gallagher, Christine Gibbons, Kay Jones, Marion Leonard, Karen O'Rourke and Georgina Young. Sincere thanks to all the people who gave up their time to give oral histories and whose stories are central to this book: Steve Allen, Eddie Amoo, Joe Ankrah, James Barton, Ian Broudie, Andy Carroll, Jayne Casey, Garry Christian, Chief Angus Chukuemeka, Sugar Deen, George Dixon, Martin Dempsey, Pete Fulwell, Norman Killon, Mike Knowler, Kof (Kofi Owusu), Connie Lush, Ian McNabb, John Power, Hilary Steele and Kathryn Williams. In addition to providing an oral history, Bill Drummond also produced a map of his Liverpool haunts and we are grateful for his permission to reproduce it in this volume. Special mention should be made of the late Lita Roza, who contributed an oral history and donated material to the original exhibition.

We would also like to acknowledge a number of useful sources of information which were drawn upon during the research process: the collections of the Institute of Popular Music, http://link2wales.co.uk and http://music-isms.blogspot.com, all of which are worth further investigation for anyone interested in the diversity of Liverpool's musical heritage. Finally, we are grateful to the multitude of people who contributed stimulating conversation, ideas, contacts and help during the research process, including Tony Bolland, Cath Bore, Mike Brocken, Sara Cohen, Ann Darby, Geoff Davies, Ed Feery, Steve Hardstaff, Steve Higginson, Ruth Hobbins at Liverpool Record Office, David Horn, Mike Jones, Mark Jordan, Dave Laing, Spencer Leigh, Rita Martelli, Alastair McKay, Mark McNulty, Gill Nightingale at Cream, Mick O'Toole, Kevin Power, Sakura, Matt Smith and Holly Tessler.

Introduction: creativity, representation and place

Robert Strachan and Marion Leonard

The opening of a themed gallery in the new Museum of Liverpool in 2011 around the idea of Liverpool as a creative city constitutes an important milestone in Liverpool's commemoration and celebration of its rich cultural heritage by what promises to be one of the world's leading city history museums. The decision to foreground this creative legacy as one of the cornerstones in the city's social history (alongside galleries dedicated to Liverpool as a people's city, port city and global city) is at the same time innovative and understandable. There is a certain inevitability that a city which has produced such a wealth of internationally renowned figures in music, literature, theatre, comedy and sport should wish to place these achievements as a central motif within its own story. This new gallery is, in fact, part of a continuity of representation whereby creativity, resourcefulness and innovation have been constant in both the way the city views itself and the way in which it has been represented on a national and international stage. In short, Liverpool both imagines and projects itself as a creative city. Within this imagining there is an underlying assumption that there is something specific about Liverpool as a place which gives rise to this creativity and has an immutable effect upon the shape it takes.

These three central themes of creativity, representation and the specificity of place constitute the fundamental core of this book and are discernible throughout its chapters. Moreover, as the title of the collection suggests, the book is also intimately concerned with the changing city and how the relationship between these three elements plays out over time. As such, it examines patterns of change and continuity within the city and how creativity has been mobilized at differing points within its history. The book thus aims to provide a critical historical account of popular music in Liverpool which explores the contextual, creative and geographical factors that have contributed to the city's status as a major centre of creativity within Anglo-American popular music. The book engages with how the city has been represented through its music and musicians, and explores both dominant and less celebrated elements of its musical history. Rather than attempting to create a singular linear account of the history of popular music and its cultures within the city, the book takes a case-study approach, centred around these thematic threads, in order to provide new perspectives on the subject.

In a general positioning piece on rock historiography Keith Negus (1997) makes the observation that there is no singular history of popular music; rather, a multitude of interweaving and sometimes conflicting histories permeate our consciousness of the past. Such a conceptualization of history underpins this volume and it very deliberately allows for multiple perspectives on a diversity of music practice throughout Liverpool's musical life. Hence, several of the chapters are based around previously unpublished oral histories or original interview research, while the remainder engage with the way in which Liverpool's music has been represented in dominant historical narratives. It is not the place of this collection to make judgements upon the veracity of individual experience or to weave the multitude of voices contained within it into a singular narrative, as if an objective version of historical truth could be constructed. Rather, it takes for granted that the experience of culture by the individual is an important facet of historical knowledge which enriches our understanding of the city's musical heritage and its wider social history.

Representation

Oral histories and interviews are valuable in offering personal reflections and insights into music practice, yet, in a city which has become world renowned for its popular music, it is important to contextualize these accounts within wider patterns of representation. Indeed, perhaps no city of its size in the world has been subject to so much scrutiny in terms of its popular culture. The unprecedented success of the Beatles has meant that narratives pertaining to the city and its music have been told and retold countless times through published histories,[1] biographies, television programmes and films.[2] In addition, representations of the city through its music and media accounts of its musicians have further concretized connections between the specificities of place and the city's creative output. It is a recurrent theme of this book that these types of representation serve to reinforce dominant historical narratives and that any critical historical approach must attempt to unpack their implicit assumptions. The book begins therefore with three chapters which explicitly address representation in differing ways.

Ian Inglis's opening chapter gets to grips with one of the fundamental framing devices that served to give Liverpool its international reputation for music: the term 'Merseybeat' itself. The chapter gives an objective and empirically grounded examination of the ways in which accounts of the city's musical sound of the early 1960s have led to a constructed notion of a Mersey sound as a coherent whole. By tracing the use and application of the term Merseybeat within media, academic and historical accounts, it considers the assumptions behind them and assesses the validity of the explanations they offer. By identifying differing strains in the way in which the term has been applied (delivery, affinity and diversity), the chapter ultimately questions the assumption that this period in the city's musical history threw up a discernible and distinct 'sound'.

In the second chapter, the well known local journalist and broadcaster Spencer Leigh offers his personal reflections on the influence of the Beatles upon the city and the experience of growing up in a city which has been so intimately connected with one of the most significant popular cultural phenomena of the second half of the twentieth century. His chapter explores the unprecedented worldwide success of the group, with particular emphasis on the effect that this has had on the city of Liverpool. It examines the ways in which the story and identity of the Beatles have been tied to the city from the time of the band's existence to the present day. Its exploration of the effect that the band's rise to fame had on people in the city during the 1960s and the way in which their story has provided an enduring cultural legacy serves to demonstrate the often conflicting attitudes engendered by the band's enormous impact.

Of course, Liverpool's wider popular music culture itself constitutes a key part of how the city is represented, a factor which is addressed in chapter 3, which deals with issues of memory and representation. The chapter traces how representations of Liverpool in song, combined with coverage of its musicians and musical cultures in broadcast media and the press, have contributed to a collective memory of the city. Using examples ranging from folk song to contemporary indie rock, the chapter traces how music and lyrics have provided a continuity of representation in relation to place. In particular, it discusses how Liverpool artists have often drawn upon the material conditions of the city (decline and social hardship for example) and the legacy of its past (as a seaport and cosmopolitan hub) for inspiration. The chapter also examines how media accounts and critical representations often contextualize the city's music and its prominent performers in very specific ways. It argues that these narratives build up in a process of historical accretion which has an active effect upon the way in which the city and its culture are understood through the constant reinforcement of a cultural legacy that is at the heart of collective memory.

Hidden histories

Given these dominant representations of the city and its musicians, the book also has a central concern with elements of musical practice which have been represented as, at best, marginal, or which have been hitherto ignored. The next three chapters of the book draw upon extensive oral history materials in order to uncover three such 'hidden' histories. By adding new narratives to, and providing new perspectives on, the historical record, all three chapters also engage with dominant strains within historiography. In their differing ways, these accounts (which take geography, race and gender as their respective foci) seek to problematize further the ways in which histories have been written and to question the ascription of importance to historical events within dominant historical narratives. These chapters reveal that despite the millions of words expended on Liverpool music, there are new stories to be told and that there is a need to take a look at well worn narratives with fresh eyes. Indeed, it is a testament to the richness of Liverpool's musical heritage that there are a multitude of hidden histories, prominent musicians and significant musical scenes that there has not been space to include within this volume. While Brocken (2010) admirably fills in many gaps relating to country, cabaret, jazz and folk, and there are a number of published personal recollections relating to a host of musical experiences within the city (McManus 1994a, 1994b; Jenkins 1994; Willis-Pitts 2000; Bolland 2006), a variety of illuminating musical practices within the city remained unstudied.

Sara Cohen and Brett Lashua's investigation into music making in the St Johns shopping precinct takes as its starting point a particular geographical location to examine strains of musical practice in the 1970s that have been marginalized in histories of the city. The musical styles (progressive rock, rhythm and blues, and heavy rock) and relative lack of commercial success of the local groups discussed in the chapter sit uneasily with the canonizing tendency of much of the history of popular music. As a result, this period has often been viewed as a time when 'nothing happened' in the city's musical life. In contrast to this dominant view, the voices contained within the chapter reveal the existence of a vibrant and creative scene which was highly significant to a generation of musicians and audiences. The chapter concentrates on three pub venues in the St Johns precinct to examine the way in which music making has been woven into the fabric of the city at differing points in its history. It also raises key issues with regard to the relationship of musical scenes to the politics of heritage and regeneration. By tracing the rise and fall of this particular cluster of musical creativity it assesses how instances of urban planning can have material effects upon music making in a given location.

Chapter 5's focus on black musicians from Liverpool goes on to address similar gaps in historical representation. Despite the commercial success of Liverpool soul acts the Real Thing in the 1970s and the Christians in the 1980s, the rich tradition of music making within Liverpool's black communities has been under-represented in historical accounts of the city's music. The chapter traces the evolution of this tradition within community institutions, such as social clubs and the church, and examines how the local specificities of immigration and cultural exchange led to the emergence of a black music scene much earlier than in other UK cities. The chapter then traces the careers of a number of musicians and vocal groups who emerged in the 1960s. It highlights significant contextual factors within the British music and media industries to explore the relative lack of commercial success of these musicians at a time when many white Liverpool groups were enjoying global fame. It then examines the eventual commercial breakthrough of the Real Thing and their influence upon the 'Brit-soul' movement of the 1970s and 1980s. Ultimately the chapter raises wider issues relating to popular music historiography. When the musicians under discussion in the chapter have been discussed, it has often been part of a revisionist tendency whereby black artists and clubs are reclaimed for their roles in relation to the development of the Beatles or Merseybeat as a whole. The chapter argues that the history of Liverpool's black musicians should be considered as an important story within itself. An examination of these musicians reveals a significant and unacknowledged strain within the history of UK black music and tells us much about the British music industry at a pivotal time in its development.

This concentration on historiography is also a central part of chapter 6, which describes how, within media accounts and previous histories, music making in Liverpool has often been represented as a male activity. Nevertheless, women have made a significant contribution in terms of commercial success within the recording industry and their involvement in local music making. The chapter examines the way in which the history of popular music has often not fully recorded the presence and contribution of women, before it draws upon new research to examine the work and experiences of Liverpool's female music makers. The chapter also deals with how female musicians have been represented within music press accounts, by drawing comparisons between coverage of Lita Roza in the 1950s and that of Abi Harding of the Zutons in the 2000s. Identifying striking similarities across a fifty-year gap, the discussion reveals how female performers are often represented in particular and gendered ways, which raises a cautionary note about drawing uncritically upon music press accounts as historical source material. The chapter concludes that oral histories can uncover important experiences of music making and musical cultures that fall outside the concerns of conventional representation.

Creativity and place

The final three chapters of the book draw together in a more explicit manner the theme of creativity and the city that runs throughout the volume. Chapters 7 and 8 examine the way in which creativity has been fostered in discrete areas of the city, while chapter 9 looks at songwriting as a creative process. These chapters deal with the creative city in differing ways: the city as a wellspring of creative activity within very specific social and geographical contexts and as a more general source of inspiration. Distinct areas of the city have been the centre of differing creative clusters within its musical life. Each of these areas has served as a location where venues, clubs, shops, rehearsal spaces and studios have emerged, creating concentrated convergencies of creative activity. In turn, the life-cycles of musical movements have been reflected in the changing look and feel of the city's urban locations, often shifting from spontaneous and seemingly chaotic spaces to models of urban regeneration. Chapters 7 and 8 are concerned with how these clusters of activity evolved and how such temporal uses of particular urban zones have had material effects upon the changing geography of the city. Both provide detailed explorations of the social and geographical contexts of the emergence of two of the city's music scenes (post-punk and house music) which would go on to garner international recognition.

Chapter 7 presents oral histories which trace the development of a number of strands within the creative scene that emerged around Mathew Street in the late 1970s. It charts the development of various institutions within the city's 'underground' cultures throughout the decade, including Liverpool Art School, Probe Records and the Liverpool School of Language, Music, Dream and Pun, before concentrating on Eric's club. The voices of key players within the scene describe how Eric's became a central focus for Liverpool's diverse underground community, fostering a creative environment which would go on to spawn a number of highly successful musicians and bands, including Orchestral Manoeuvres in the Dark, Echo and the Bunnymen, the Teardrop Explodes and Frankie Goes to Hollywood. The oral histories contained within the chapter ultimately reveal a bohemian thread in the city's culture where fashion, art, design, theatre and music intersected. As such, they give a rich portrait of an environment where ideas became cross-fertilized across artistic boundaries and are an important example of how social and geographical factors can lead to new creative trajectories.

The significance of place upon popular music practice is addressed in a slightly different way in Georgina Young's following chapter on house music in Liverpool. It describes how electronic dance music (a music characterized by its global connections) became inscribed with a highly localized resonance for many of its participants. It traces the history of house music's shifting locations across the city to explore a changing relationship to the city's geography and culture. From *ad hoc* warehouse raves through to Quadrant Park, the UK's first legal acid house all-nighter, and the emergence of Cream as a global brand, the chapter examines how club culture in the late 1980s and 1990s served to change the city's cultural and physical landscape. The chapter illustrates how creative work within popular music cultures is also undertaken by business people and audiences. In this instance the creative city became manifest through the innovation of promoters and entrepreneurs, harnessing the vibrancy of club culture to transform areas of the city from a post-industrial shell to a hub of the night-time economy.

The final chapter, on Liverpool songwriters, raises more general questions about creativity and popular music, before discussing how the specificities of place have had an effect upon the practices of songwriters from the city. The chapter examines the nature of musical creativity itself through an exploration of how individual imaginative ideas, which are central to the creative process, are shaped by accumulated knowledge about musical structures and conventions. Using interviews with a variety of Liverpool songwriters the chapter outlines differing elements of the songwriting process in terms of inspiration, craft and collaboration. The chapter concludes with an echo of the first three chapters of the book by addressing how Liverpool's musical legacy has affected these songwriters in differing, and sometimes conflicting, ways.

While all of the chapters in the book illustrate a rich musical heritage, they also reveal Liverpool as a changing city, constantly evolving and throwing up new opportunities and challenges to its creative communities. The processes of change within the city have had undeniable effects upon its musical output and doubtless will continue to do so. The city is an environment of possibility which engenders cycles of creative change, where Liverpool's musical legacy is subject to new interpretation and changing patterns within its urban spaces, resulting in a series of shifting bohemias. For example, Wolstenholme Square, once the centre of Liverpool's dance music scene in the heyday of Cream, is now the home of a vibrant art and music scene evident in new venues which have sprung up in its disused spaces. The Kazimir (located at the site of a long-abandoned nightclub on the square) has established itself as the centre for a new generation of underground musicians, cabaret artists and actors. Mello Mello (once the pre-club haunt of Liverpool's clubbers) now showcases a rotating collection of Liverpool's DIY musicians, sound artists, poets and performers, while the Wolstenholme Projects (located in another disused building, opposite the Kazimir) hosts a variety of screenings, visual art exhibitions and happenings. It remains to be seen what lasting legacy these new creative alliances will engender and this transient scene will, in time, undoubtedly dissipate and regroup, perhaps transforming other areas of the urban landscape. Such a transience should not be mourned, however, as it is a mixture of transience and tradition that are at the heart of Liverpool as a creative city. Locations and people will inevitably change, new scenes will supersede old ones, and the musical heritage described in this collection will no doubt be mined in innovative and unforeseen ways by future generations of the city's musicians.

Notes

1   The on-line retailer Amazon, for instance, lists over 16,000 titles relating to the Beatles in its book section.
2   For example, *The Hours and Times* (1991), *Backbeat* (1994), *Across the Universe* (2007) and *Nowhere Boy* (2009).

References

Bolland, Tony (2006) *Plug Inn (The Forgotten Years)*. Liverpool: Bolland and Lowe.

Brocken, Michael (2010) *Other Voices: Hidden Histories of Liverpool's Popular Music Scenes, 1930s–1970s*. Aldershot: Ashgate.

Jenkins, Tricia (1994) *'Let's Go Dancing': Dance Band Memories of 1930s Liverpool*. Liverpool: Institute of Popular Music.

McManus, Kevin (1994a) *Nashville of the North: Country Music in Liverpool*. Liverpool: Institute of Popular Music.

McManus, Kevin (1994b) *Céilís, Jigs and Ballads: Irish Music in Liverpool.* Liverpool: Institute of Popular Music.

Negus, Keith (1997) *Popular Music in Theory.* London: Polity.

Willis-Pitts, P (2000) *Liverpool, the 5th Beatle: An African American Odyssey.* Littleton, CO: Amozen Press.

CHAPTER I

Historical approaches to Merseybeat: delivery, affinity and diversity

Ian Inglis

Introduction

This chapter examines connections between Liverpool as a city and the Mersey sound, or, as it has been frequently labelled, 'Merseybeat'. Even a cursory inspection of the history of popular music reveals that perceptions of an association between music and place are frequent and unremarkable. Indeed, there are so many attempts to describe and define musical styles by containing them within a geographical category that it could be argued the practice has become less a convention than a cliché. But does this routine exercise in labelling reflect the existence of authentic causal connections between a city's social practices and its music? Or is it merely a shorthand device for naming and marketing musical outputs that actually have very little in common other than their point of origin?

The emergence of Merseybeat as a term is significant, in that it represented, in 1963, the first time in the history of British popular music when a sound and a city were bracketed together in this way. Of course, the notion of Merseybeat was built, initially at least, around the early successes of the Beatles, and as their career expanded the term became familiar not just in the UK but also to global audiences. The chapter examines the ways in which accounts of the city's musical sound in the early 1960s have been presented. It considers the assumptions behind those accounts, assesses the validity of the explanations they offer and traces the evolution of academic, journalistic and populist discourses about Merseybeat. The contributions can be organized into three categories (delivery, affinity and diversity), which are broadly distinctive perspectives that usefully indicate the different ways in which the sound of Merseybeat has been approached. My concern is not to prove or deny the existence of a specific sound. Nor am I arguing that Merseybeat itself – whatever that may have been – was subject to evolution and transformation. My focus is merely to investigate the manner in which the sound of the Beatles and their peers in the late 1950s and early 1960s was heard, analysed and explained by different commentators at different times, and to understand the way in which the concept of Merseybeat has been theorized.

UK popular music before Merseybeat

After the emergence of rock'n'roll in the United States in the early 1950s, popular music was something which arrived in Britain from across the Atlantic. US performers like Elvis Presley, the Everly Brothers, Connie Francis, Brenda Lee, Pat Boone and Roy Orbison dominated the radio stations, the jukeboxes, the dance halls and the pages of the weekly popular music press. In 1956, there were twelve number one singles in the UK: ten of these were American and just two were British; in 1957, of thirteen number one singles, nine were American and four British; in 1958, there were again thirteen number one singles, of which eleven were American and two British.

What British performers there were tended to model themselves very closely on their US counterparts: Cliff Richard and Billy Fury were passable copies of Elvis Presley; Adam Faith was an imitator of Buddy Holly; and Craig Douglas replicated Pat Boone. In addition, there were very few groups; it was an unwritten rule that 'pop stars' – who were predominantly white, of course – were solo performers. Even when groups were featured, their billing explicitly maintained an appropriate distinction between lead singer and backing musicians: Cliff Richard and the Shadows, Joe Brown and the Bruvvers, Marty Wilde and the Wildcats, the Karl Denver Trio, Johnny Kidd and the

Pirates, and so on. Furthermore, the popular music industry was based exclusively and inevitably in London; it was utterly implausible to seek to pursue a musical career from outside the capital. Indeed, one of the reasons why the Decca record label rejected the Beatles in 1962 was that it opted instead for the safety and convenience of signing the London-based Brian Poole and the Tremeloes, who also conformed to the model of lead singer and backing group.

In the late 1950s and early 1960s, there seemed little reason to believe that any of this might change, or that performers and audiences in Britain might break free from their duplication and consumption of US music. Consequently, there had been no suggestions of connections between British music and specific places: with no, or very little, distinctive British music, even talk of a British sound was rather illogical. By contrast, analyses of the development of popular music in the United States had long been constructed around the clear recognition of specific regional variations. Gillett (1971: 29–44) for instance, identifies distinct musical strands related to place that coalesced in the early 1950s.

Delivery: the Hamburg sound

The only significant exception to the postwar US dominance of British popular music was the success of skiffle music in the mid-1950s. Skiffle was a peculiarly British combination of US blues, folk and jazz traditions. Its leading performer was Lonnie Donegan, and its simple and inexpensive equipment (guitar, banjo, double bass, washboard and drums) had persuaded many youngsters in Britain to engage in a positional shift or switch, that is, to move from music listening to music making. Although it lasted only for two or three years, the skiffle boom was a crucial element in the development of British music. As Coleman (1984: 50) has noted:

> Donegan's influence on British popular music was incalculable. He had a basic three-chord style, easy to copy, and the line-up of his group inspired hundreds of thousands of young people to make do-it-yourself music.

Those inspired included: George Harrison, whose musical debut was as a member of the Rebels, a skiffle group formed by Harrison and his elder brother Pete in 1956; Ringo Starr, who was a member of the Eddie Clayton Skiffle Group from 1957 to 1958; and John Lennon, who in July 1957 invited Paul McCartney to join the Quarrymen skiffle group.

Lennon's group (composed of friends from Quarry Bank High School) was typical of the response to skiffle in Liverpool. In many ways, it represented – like punk, twenty years later – a democratization of music, in that it allowed youngsters who were not musically trained or instrumentally gifted, or who lacked the money to buy expensive equipment, to make music. It has been estimated that by the early 1960s there were around 400 semi-professional groups – no longer playing skiffle – working in the city; and some of these also made frequent appearances in Hamburg, after club-owners Bruno Koschmider and Peter Eckhorn had begun to recruit groups from Liverpool for their venues around the Reeperbahn in 1960. This is a key point: the phenomenon of Merseybeat did not suddenly appear overnight in 1963 when the Beatles made their chart breakthrough, but had been in existence for several years through groups like the Searchers, the Swinging Blue Jeans, Cass and the Casanovas, Gerry and the Pacemakers, the Big Three, the Fourmost, Kingsize Taylor and the Dominoes, Rory Storm and the Hurricanes, the Merseybeats, the Undertakers, the Remo Four, Derry and the Seniors, and Faron's Flamingos.

In addition to the impetus provided by skiffle, there were two other relevant factors at work in this musical growth. First, there was, among British audiences, a general disappointment with the reluctance of many leading US performers to visit Britain, and their unwillingness to appear outside London if and when they did visit. Secondly, there had been a decline in the energy and showmanship of the rock'n'roll of the mid-1950s, as the industry sought to regain its control over commercial music. By promoting entertainers like Bobby Vee, Paul Anka, Bobby Rydell, Ricky Nelson, Frankie Avalon, Fabian, Gene Pitney and Bobby Vinton, all of whom were perceived as much 'safer' options than earlier examples like Little Richard, Jerry Lee Lewis, Larry Williams, Chuck Berry and Gene Vincent, rock'n'roll was effectively replaced by a smoother, tamer, more polite variant, which Cohn (1969: 52–57) has called 'highschool' and Shaw (1992: 107) has labelled the era of 'the "teen idol" … [when] music left the streets and moved to the studios'.

Faced with this situation, the response of many British teenagers was to move from the consumption of music to its creation. As Harker (1980: 75) notes, 'the commercially dead period around 1960 was one of the most potent and creative times for British adolescent working-class musical culture'. The early accounts of that music – mainly at first hand, from a time when they were performing to small, local audiences in Liverpool and Hamburg – focus less on interior characteristics (the music itself) and more on exterior characteristics (its delivery or the manner of its performance). In particular, the ability to generate excitement on stage was consistently highlighted as the single most important element.

For example, Allan Williams, who acted as the Beatles' *de facto* manager in 1960–61, wrote of their impact in the summer of 1960:

> When the Beatles came on, it was as though someone had pressed ever so gently on the nervous system of each and every boy and girl in that hall.... They gave off an animal charge which wound up the audience like a tight watch spring. Then *wham!* The spring was re-leased and it all hung out, emotion spilled over, swamped the Beatles and engulfed them.... There was something supernatural about it. (Williams and Marshall 1975: 139)

It was also noted by Astrid Kirchherr, the young German art student who would later become Stuart Sutcliffe's girlfriend, when she saw the Beatles (Lennon, McCartney, Harrison, Sutcliffe and Pete Best) in November 1960:

> When I first met the Beatles in the Kaiserkeller in Hamburg, it was immediately clear to me that they were something very special.... Their unbelievable stage presence struck me with tremendous power. Their musicality, their good looks, and their spot-on humour.... They attracted us like human magnets. (Sawyers 2006: xv)

Her recollections are supported by an account of the Beatles in Hamburg from Ulf Kruger, German musician and songwriter:

> the rock'n'roll numbers went down particularly well on account of their irrepressible energy.... The Beatles took off like rockets with their cool humour, their magical stage presence, and their electrify-ing music delivered with raw energy. (Kruger 2006: 82–85)

Liverpool promoter Sam Leach's account of the Beatles in January 1961 also emphasized their charismatic presence:

> What I saw and heard next will be etched forever on my mind.... The decomposing curtains fell apart and the five animated lads dressed in black bounced into my life.... Everyone was enraptured. Adjectives haven't been coined that do justice to the spine-tingling performance I witnessed that first night.... It was awesome. (Leach 1999: 46)

And Brian Epstein's account of his initial visit to the Cavern in November 1961 noted again the performative element of the show:

> I had never seen anything like the Beatles on any stage.... They turned their backs on the audience and shouted at them and laughed at private jokes. But they gave a captivating and honest show and they had very considerable magnetism.... There was quite clearly an excitement in the otherwise unpleasant dungeon which was quite removed from any of the formal entertainments provided at places like the Liverpool Empire or the London Palladium. (Epstein 1964: 44)

All the above accounts say next to nothing about the group's music. There is, in fact, general agreement among the commentators of this period that the roots of this sound – a *visual* sound, rather than an *aural* sound – lay in the professional experiences of Liverpool groups in Hamburg. To satisfy the often rowdy German audiences' demands for entertainment, and to develop a reputation for providing more exciting shows than competing venues, the performers were urged by their employers to engage in distinctive and memorable stagecraft. Clayson has claimed that the Liverpool groups quickly learned to be

> less concerned with technical accuracy than the generation of a lively all-night party atmosphere to foster a rapid turnover at the counter, and defuse potential unrest.... Competition between musicians to outdo one another's stage antics was matched by that for business between the clubs they served. (Clayson 1997: 70)

As Davies (1968: 87) concluded, '*making show*, as the Germans called it, was the vital thing'.

Thus, while these pre-1963 references to Merseybeat may attest to a Liverpool (or Hamburg) *style*, there is very little evidence of a Liverpool *sound*; if there is, it is evident in its delivery. Performance, stagecraft and delivery are the crucial constituents. This should not be surprising. After all, with no examples of recorded music to hear and to assess, the only way in which the Beatles and others could be evaluated was through what they did – through the sounds they produced – on stage.

Affinity: the Liverpool sound

The Beatles' first single, 'Love Me Do', was a minor success in the autumn of 1962. Their breakthrough came in 1963, when they achieved four number one singles in Britain and two number one albums. By the end of the year, there had been significant chart successes for other Liverpool performers, including the Searchers, Gerry and the Pacemakers, Billy J. Kramer and the Dakotas, the Big Three, the Swinging Blue Jeans and the Fourmost. The following year, in what became known as the 'British invasion', the pattern was repeated in the United States and around the world, following the Beatles' American television debut on *The Ed Sullivan Show*; at one point in March 1964, the group famously occupied the top five positions in *Billboard* magazine's singles chart. The term Beatlemania was coined to describe the scenes of mass hysteria that accompanied their appearances, and musicians, journalists and musicologists attempted to explain the Liverpool groups' remarkable successes by searching for some common element, or affinity, in their music.

Many of these investigations centred around the Beatles, but the fact that other performers from a city that had previously contributed little or nothing should, within the space of a few months, so completely dominate much of the world's popular music convinced many that there was not just a Beatles sound, but a Liverpool sound. And, very quickly, the emphasis in these explanations switched from performance to music – from form to content. A common assumption was that the sound of their music – cover versions and self-compositions alike – was, in fact, a combination of different sounds and styles that were mainly American in origin. Gillett, for example, decided that it was

> a derivative of two American styles which had not previously been put together, the hard rock and roll style of singers like Little Richard and Larry Williams, and the soft gospel call-and-response style of the Shirelles, the Drifters, and the rest of the singers produced by Leiber and Stoller, Luther Dixon, and Berry Gordy. (Gillett 1971: 309)

Producer George Martin, whose artists included not only the Beatles but also Gerry and the Pacemakers, Billy J. Kramer and the Dakotas, and the Fourmost, offered a similar explanation:

It was the result of combining all the elements of American pop – not just rock'n'roll and rhythm and blues, but girl groups, and Motown too. The Beatles had half a dozen girl group covers on their first two LPs; the Mersey sound of fellow performers ... depended on the American pop use of vocal harmonies. (Martin 1983: 31)

And a similar, if rather more complex, analysis of parts has been provided by Friedlander:

classic rock numbers from Chuck Berry, Little Richard and Buddy Holly; rhythm and blues tunes from Ray Charles, Larry Williams, the Isley Brothers, and Leiber and Stoller; Carl Perkins rockabilly songs; early 1960s American pop tunes from Carole King and Motown; and an assortment of British pop tunes. (Friedlander 1996: 83)

Why music making in Liverpool rather than Manchester, Sheffield, Newcastle, Birmingham, Leeds or Glasgow should have been so susceptible to the impact and influence of American sounds was explained by the city's status as Britain's principal transatlantic port – a point of first contact with America. Among the shipping lines based in Liverpool were Cunard and Canadian Pacific. They provided jobs for many thousands of Liverpudlians, and the ability of these 'Cunard Yanks' to regularly cross the Atlantic and return to the city with clothes, accessories, fashions, comics and – crucially – records not widely available in Britain created a distinctive musical and cultural network that aspiring musicians were able to access. John McNally, rhythm guitarist with the Searchers, explained that:

Most people in Liverpool had some relation who went to sea, and could bring record imports in. My brother bought me Hank Williams records first of all and I started from there.... He brought back the first Elvis ones, then Carl Perkins, then Buddy Holly, long before they were released over here. I remember him coming over and saying he'd seen Elvis on the telly and Jerry Lee Lewis live. (Leigh 2004: 31)

So, as the Beatles biographer Philip Norman described:

While Britain listened to Adam Faith and 'pop', Liverpool listened to rhythm and blues.... All over Merseyside each Saturday night, in ballrooms, town halls, Co-op halls, even swimming baths and ice-skating rinks, there were amateur R&B groups playing Chuck Berry songs, Little Richard, Fats Domino and B. B. King songs which, filtered through a Scouse accent, did not depart much in spirit from the original. (Norman 1981: 56)

But, if Liverpool was not the only transatlantic port in Britain – London and Southampton, after all, also had strong American connections – why should it be the one where American musical patterns were so deeply embedded? Everett has suggested that it was the influence of one man, Bob Wooler, the compere at the Cavern from 1960 to 1967 and a disc jockey at many other venues around the city, who was the first to realize the value of the unique musical advantage the city enjoyed:

> More important than any other single influence, the city centre of Liverpool was blessed with Bob Wooler, a self-described 'dee-jay/ compere' who would go from club to club playing requests from his extensive collection of American records between sets of live entertainment. This led to the Liverpool 'beat scene'.... A new musical culture, created by dozens of popular bands in the city centre and hundreds of them in the outlying districts. (Everett 2001: 39)

The claim for a decisive musical affinity, spanning the many groups who performed in Liverpool and Hamburg, has also been made by Spitz:

> It was, from beginning to end, a Liverpool phenomenon. There was no mistaking that a distinctive sound was developing: chord patterns that repeated in their repertoires, a penchant for exquisitely modulated phrasing and sudden downshifting into minor chords, deliberate Everly Brothers references in the harmonies, ways of punctuating lyrics with dynamics, all of it creating a unique, idiosyncratic pop style ... identified the world over as the Liverpool or Mersey sound. (Spitz 2005: 308)

And, in addition to the sounds of American soul, rhythm'n'blues and country, to which the city was accustomed, there was yet another demographic advantage that worked its way into the music. As Kozinn has pointed out:

> The city also had a more colourful ethnic make-up than many other English cities at the time. There was a large Irish population, as well as sizeable Jamaican, Indian, Chinese, Slavic and Jewish communities, making Liverpool the kind of cultural melting-pot that New York was and London was not. These influences, both individually and in their mixture, can be heard tellingly. (Kozinn 1995: 16)

This approach also offers a startlingly simple explanation of the huge success of the Beatles and other Liverpool performers in the

United States: the music they produced was nothing more than an appropriation and reassembly of the familiar musical sounds of North America itself. Marcus has argued that when American audiences were confronted with a sound that recycled and recalled a vast range of 1950s and 1960s US performers and composers, they were attracted, in part, by an underlying familiarity:

> Accompanying the shock of novelty so many experienced on first exposure to the Beatles in 1963 or 1964 was a shock of recognition, which bespoke the Beatles' connection to the whole history of rock and roll up to that time. The Beatles had absorbed that history – year by year, playing and listening and writing. (Marcus 1992: 218)

It should be noted, however, that there was another, less common, reading of the Liverpool sound, which equated it with English rather than American traditions. In his celebrated review in *The Times* at the end of 1963, the paper's music critic, William Mann, argued that:

> For several decades, in fact since the decline of the music-hall, England has taken her popular songs from the United States, either directly or by mimicry. But the songs of Lennon and McCartney are distinctly indigenous in character, the most imaginative and inventive examples of a style that has been developing on Merseyside during the past few years. (Mann 1963)

And that analysis has been supported by Paraire:

> Musicians like the Beatles developed a new kind of music, which was closer to English popular music, with its Welsh and Scottish roots, and its melodic traditions and choral work, reminiscent of traditional English folk.... They developed a new sound, the distinctively pure and clear 'Liverpool sound'. (Paraire 1990: 68, 83)

In any event, whether the ingredients were perceived as English, British, American, or all three, within the years of Beatlemania, efforts to isolate the components of a generic sound switched from its delivery or its performance to its specific musical personality. And the dominant explanation was to see that musical personality as a synthesis of existing sounds, live and on record, that were 'saturated with intertextuality' (Weinstein 1998: 141). Thus, this perspective saw a specific and unique Liverpool sound that reflected an affinity, or similarity, between the groups from that city; and the Beatles were merely a part of that shared sound.

Diversity: the Beatles sound

One can plausibly argue that if there was something called Mersey-beat, it had disappeared by 1966: the Beatles and their management had effectively and permanently moved to London – both personally and professionally – by the end of 1963, which increasingly compli-cated the identification of them as a uniquely Liverpool group; many of those Liverpool groups which had been successful from 1963 up to 1966 found it difficult to sustain that success and gradually became less visible; and, of course, the Beatles' decision in 1966 to stop tour-ing in order to concentrate on studio work was a decisive shift away from the tradition of a performance-based popular music career.

And following the band members' increasing involvement in solo projects, it was the formal announcement of the Beatles' split in 1970 that finally signalled the end of an active Liverpudlian presence in musical practice. Since then, there has grown up a considerable industry (biographical and academic) devoted to deconstructing and reconstructing the significance of Merseybeat in general and the career of the Beatles in particular, and their places within the history of popular culture. I want now to consider what fresh in-sights or perspectives such accounts may have brought – with the benefit of several decades of reflection and hindsight – to analyses of Merseybeat and the way in which those assessments differ from the two approaches discussed above.

Perhaps the first thing to note is that the status of the Beatles has transformed almost beyond belief in the last thirty or forty years. Before 1963, they were simply a locally based rock'n'roll group, popular in Liverpool and Hamburg, but unknown elsewhere. Then, from 1963 to 1966, they had huge successes around the world: their voices and faces were the most recognized symbols of the 'swinging sixties' and they became – and remain – the iconic images of the decade. But since the late 1960s, the group has been subject to a persistent re-evaluation that extends far outside its musical context, along several parallel dimensions.

- Economically, the Beatles (and their Liverpool peers) are seen as largely responsible for the evolution of popular music in Britain from a small branch of the domestic entertainment business into one of the country's most profitable exports.

- Musically, they introduced innovative elements into the composition and construction of their songs that served as examples for others to follow.
- Industrially, they asserted an independence that helped to free them, and others, from the restrictive and paternalistic patterns of management and organization that had characterized the music business in Britain.
- Historically, the group is perceived as one of the key moments in the narrative of the twentieth century.
- Politically, they demonstrated that entertainers may also be permitted to step into the role of intellectuals.
- Socially, their unprecedented global popularity was achieved in part by the capacity that they, and their music, possessed to overcome traditional distinctions of nationality, age, gender and social class among communities of fans.
- Culturally, they shifted the consumption, discussion and analysis of popular music into settings from which it had been previously excluded.

Assessments of their music and career are, inevitably, coloured by these factors, but it is important to concentrate on those commentaries which have focused on the question of sound. In fact, clues to the direction of many of the post-Beatles reflections and assessments can be found in some relatively early accounts. In the mid-1960s, Leslie asked:

> What is it, then, that is so different, so dynamic, about this music? What can be heard seems to be just a group of boys singing, sometimes in unison, sometimes in harmony, while they accompany themselves on guitars and drums. Just that. The specifically Merseyside aspect of the sound has, in the interests of ballyhoo, been overstressed. (Leslie 1965: 134–35)

And further doubt on the existence of a unified and common sound came from the jazz musician and writer George Melly (1970: 75), who commented that, by the end of 1963, 'the Beatles ... were still thought of as a part of "the Liverpool sound". Whether the Liverpool sound existed is another matter'.

Such disruptions to the conventional wisdom of a Liverpool sound were unusual in accounts written in the 1960s, but in recent years they have become more familiar. Writing twenty years after the onset of Beatlemania, O'Grady directly questioned the existence of a coherent Mersey sound by arguing that much of the Beatles' music actually had more in common with groups from London:

> By 1964, the Searchers and the Hollies, both worked in the pop-rock style of Gerry and the Pacemakers, without the intensity and harmonic variety associated with the Beatles. However, two English groups do demonstrate the influence of the Beatles in this period: the Dave Clark Five, whose 'Glad All Over' echoes the call and response style of the Beatles; and Manfred Mann, whose 'Do Wah Diddy Diddy' also incorporates aspects of the Beatles' vocal style. (O'Grady 1983: 175–76)

And Bradley noted differences rather than similarities in the sounds produced by the city's groups:

> One of the most striking things about 'Merseybeat' was the great variety ... King Size Taylor and the Dominoes were producing fairly good imitation rock'n'roll from as early as 1957, others like Ian and the Zodiacs and Gerry and the Pacemakers were covering rock-pop tunes from the USA and the British charts, and even experimenting with writing their own, Faron's Flamingos were working on soul-type sounds, Sonny Webb and the Cascades were doing rockabilly and country songs [and] the Swinging Blue Jeans began as a trad jazz group in the late 1950s. (Bradley 1992: 75)

These, and other, contributions suggest that there was in fact no common sound or style that united its performers. What there may have been, however, was a 'disposition' or 'sensibility'. Assessing those Liverpool groups which were successful in America, Bangs (1992: 202) suggested that 'the British Invasion was more important as an event, as a *mood*, than as music.... The groups that made it in the United States provide the various colours that comprise that mood'.

McKeen (1989: 78–79) reached a similar conclusion in his historical assessment of the Beatles and their music:

> The Beatles were announcing that the Beatles were not just a rock and roll group, but an attitude or a movement ... to measure their influence merely in terms of music is to diminish it. As much as anything else the Beatles symbolized an attitude. (McKeen 1989: 78–79)

Of course, the city of Liverpool itself has been more than happy to support the idea of a distinctive, and familiar, sound. Gould has suggested that within the city's traditional working-class social and occupational communities, where excessive individuality was inherently suspect, there was a tendency to seek out explanations and activities that stressed a communal, or collective, culture. But, he argues, while the idea of a common musical sound was an attractive and convenient version of events, it was simply wrong to equate the sounds of the Beatles with the sounds produced by other Liverpool performers: 'No other local group sounded like them, looked like them, or behaved like them' (Gould 2007: 111–12).

Mellers has also stressed the differences rather than the similarities of the music produced by Liverpool groups. While the Beatles 'knew the right time and place to be born [and] the local, the American and the cosmopolitan were inextricably intertwined' (Mellers 1973: 31–32) these factors alone are not sufficient to explain their music. The crucial question to be asked is: what did the Beatles (and others) bring to the rock experience *themselves*? What they brought, Mellers asserted, was a whole variety of individual ambitions, talents, attitudes and motivations, some musical, some non-musical – expressed in very different, often highly individualistic ways. The popular historical construction of a recognizable sound thus becomes a flawed exercise, since it overlooks the performers' inherent diversity and attempts to impose a common structure and unity where none existed. And this is just as true of the early Beatles (the Beatles of 'Love Me Do', 'She Loves You' and 'I Want To Hold Your Hand') as it is of the later Beatles (the Beatles of *Revolver*, *Sgt. Pepper* and *Magical Mystery Tour*).

Conclusion

These alternative approaches present a series of conceptual shifts, moving from an assessment in which the concept of Merseybeat is contained within an emphasis on its delivery or performance, to a position which sees a Liverpool sound as the distinctive consequence of patterns of generic musical intertextuality, to a counter-argument which questions the existence of a Liverpool sound *per se* by emphasizing its diversity rather than its unity. What are we to make of all this?

As already indicated, there is no doubt that the concept of Merseybeat was enormously attractive. As well as being a succinct marketing brand, it also supplied a convenient label that could be employed and exploited by a fascinated and hungry news media, for which the global success of the Beatles, or of any British popular music or musicians, was an unprecedented event, and which lacked the experience, expertise or conceptual tools with which to make sense of it. But as critical, media and academic expertise and experience grew, initially through the 1960s, and into the 1970s, 1980s, 1990s and beyond, the shorthand vocabulary of Merseybeat came to be seen as a wholly inadequate description of the varieties of music the city produced.

It may be significant that very few systematic attempts were made at the time (or, indeed, have been made since) to identify the existence of a distinct sound in other British cities. The Who, the Yardbirds, the Kinks, the Small Faces, Manfred Mann, the Dave Clark Five, the Rolling Stones and the Pretty Things were among the internationally successful groups to emerge from London in the mid-1960s, yet there has been no comparable investigation of a 'London sound'. This was because the popular music industry in Britain saw London-based success as normal and predictable. It did not need to be explained. When, against all expectations, significant successes, led by the Beatles, started to emanate from Liverpool – typically regarded as a city in decline, a cultural wasteland, peripherally located at the other side of the country – a plausible account had to be constructed. The solution was the alleged 'discovery' of a previously unknown sound. And this provided a simple explanation for what might have otherwise remained an embarrassing and unexpected challenge to the supremacy of London as the centre of creative entertainment.

This does not undermine the argument that social and musical networks are influenced by time and place. They are, in just the same way that any other set of cultural practices (sport, art, dance, theatre) are influenced by the same forces. Cohen's (1995: 444) claim that 'music reflects social, economic, political and material aspects of the place in which it is created' is correct. But those aspects will not necessarily be reflected in exactly the same way for everyone involved. And, in the same way that music is informed by time and place, so too is musical commentary equally informed by time and place. This discussion has shown that the nature of the associations between music and place can be, and have been, critically interpreted in different ways. In the case of the Beatles and Merseybeat, those interpretations have been historically manifested in terms of a focus on its *delivery* or performance, on its *affinity*, through the existence of a Liverpool sound, and on its *diversity*, and the uniqueness of the Beatles sound.

An important, but neglected, option in musical analysis is to listen to what performers and musicians themselves have to say. At a press conference in Paris in 1963, when asked about the Liverpool sound, George Harrison replied:

> We don't like to call it anything. The critics and the people who write about it have to call it something. They didn't want to say it was rock'n'roll, because that was supposed to have gone out about five years ago ... and they decided it wasn't really rhythm'n'blues. So they called it the Liverpool Sound, which is stupid really. (Giuliano and Giuliano 1995: 6)

Perhaps the last word should go to John Lennon, asked for his thoughts on the subject in 1964:

> We don't think there is such a thing as the Mersey Sound. That's just something journalists cooked up, a name. It just so happened we came from Liverpool, and they looked for the nearest river and named it. (Beatles 2000: 101)

References

Bangs, Lester (1992) 'The British Invasion'. In: Anthony DeCurtis and James Henke (eds) *The Rolling Stone Illustrated History of Rock & Roll*. London: Plexus. pp. 199–208.

Beatles (2000) *The Beatles Anthology*. London: Cassell.

Bradley, Dick (1992) *Understanding Rock'n'Roll*. Buckingham: Open University Press.

Clayson, Alan (1997) *Hamburg: The Cradle Of British Rock*. London: Sanctuary.

Cohen, Sara (1995) 'Sounding Out the City: Music and the Sensuous Production of Place'. *Transactions of the Institute of British Geographers* 20: 434–46.

Cohn, Nik (1969) *Awopbopaloobop Alopbamboom*. London: Weidenfeld and Nicholson.

Coleman, Ray (1984) *John Lennon*. London: Sidgwick and Jackson.

Davies, Hunter (1968) *The Beatles*. London: Heinemann.

Epstein, Brian (1964) *A Cellarful of Noise*. London: Souvenir Press.

Everett, Walter (2001) *The Beatles as Musicians: The Quarry Men Through Rubber Soul*. Oxford: Oxford University Press.

Friedlander, Paul (1996) *Rock and Roll: A Social History*. Boulder, CO: Westview.

Gillett, Charlie (1971) *The Sound of the City*. London: Sphere Books.

Giuliano, Geoffrey and Brenda Giuliano (1995) *The Lost Beatles Interviews*. London: Virgin.

Gould, Jonathan (2007) *Can't Buy Me Love: The Beatles, Britain, and America*. New York: Harmony Books.

Harker, Dave (1980) *One for the Money*. London: Hutchinson.

Kozinn, Allan (1995) *The Beatles*. London: Phaidon.

Kruger, Ulf (2006) 'Rock'n'Roll + Skiffle = Beat'. In: Ulf Kruger and Ortwin Pelc (eds) *The Hamburg Sound*. Hamburg: Ellert and Richter. pp. 76–85.

Leach, Sam (1999) *The Rocking City*. Gwynned: Pharoah Press.

Leigh, Spencer (2004) *Twist and Shout: Merseybeat, the Cavern, the Star Club and the Beatles*. Liverpool: Nirvana.

Leslie, Peter (1965) *Fab: The Anatomy of a Phenomenon*. London: MacGibbon and Kee.

Mann, William (1963) 'What Songs the Beatles Sang'. *The Times*, 27 December. p. 4.

Marcus, Greil (1992) 'The Beatles'. In: Anthony DeCurtis and James Henke (eds) *The Rolling Stone Illustrated History of Rock & Roll*. London: Plexus. pp. 209–22.

Martin, George (1983) *Making Music*. London: Pan.

McKeen, William (1989) *The Beatles: A Bio-Bibliography*. New York: Greenwood Press.

Mellers, Wilfrid (1973) *Twilight of the Gods: The Beatles in Retrospect*. London: Faber and Faber.

Melly, George (1970) *Revolt Into Style*. London: Allen Lane.

Norman, Philip (1981) *Shout! The True Story of the Beatles*. London: Hamish Hamilton.

O'Grady, Terence J. (1983) *The Beatles: A Musical Evolution*. Boston, MA: Twayne.

Paraire, Philippe (1990) *50 Years of Rock Music*. Paris: Bordas.

Sawyers, June Skinner (ed.) (2006) *Read the Beatles*. London: Penguin.

Shaw, Greg (1992) 'The Teen Idols'. In: Anthony DeCurtis and James Henke (eds) *The Rolling Stone Illustrated History of Rock & Roll*. London: Plexus. pp. 107–12.

Spitz, Bob (2005) *The Beatles*. New York: Little, Brown.

Weinstein, Donna (1998) 'The History of Rock's Past Through Rock Covers'. In: Thomas Swiss, John Sloop and Andrew Herman (eds) *Mapping the Beat: Popular Music and Contemporary Theory*. London: Blackwell. pp. 137–51.

Williams, Allan and William Marshall (1975) *The Man Who Gave the Beatles Away*. London: Elm Tree Books.

CHAPTER 2

Growing up with the Beatles

Spencer Leigh

Introduction

This chapter explores the phenomenal worldwide success of the Beatles and the effect that this has had on the city of Liverpool. It examines the ways in which the story and identity of the Beatles have been tied to the city from the time of the band's existence to the present day. It also looks at the effect that the band's rise to fame had on people in the city during the 1960s and the way in which their story has provided an enduring cultural legacy.

If there had been such an accolade as European Capital of Culture in 1962, everybody would have laughed at a nomination of Liverpool and the title surely would have gone elsewhere. Many of the civic and commercial buildings were first rate; the Liverpool Royal Philharmonic Orchestra was world class and the Walker Art Gallery was showing initiative with the exhibition of entries for the John Moores Contemporary Painting Prize, but it probably would not be enough for a winning bid. Even in 2003, when the winner was about to be announced for 2008, it was by no means clear that Liverpool would be successful, although I was confident. My reasoning was simple: in the intervening years accepted definitions of culture had shifted to allow both football and popular music to form part of the bid. With rock music in the package, what chance did a rival bid from Birmingham have? How could Ozzy Osbourne compete with the Beatles?

The majority of successful acts have fans who attend their concerts and buy their CDs; if they are fortunate, they make hit records that are known by the population as a whole, perhaps even internationally. The success of the Beatles is way, way beyond that, though, as their influence is everywhere: in film (the quasi-documentary *A Hard Day's Night*), in fashion (mop-top haircuts, collarless jackets, Beatle boots), in promoting Eastern religions and music (sitars, the Maharishi), in encouraging foreign trade (the grounds for their MBEs), in handling the media (witty press conferences) and, naturally, in music (innovative record packaging, new recording techniques). The Beatles' predominance leaves even Elvis Presley behind.

Before the Beatles, popular music had been principally an American art form and British musicians and songwriters had, with few exceptions, been poor cousins. The Beatles' worldwide domination gave the UK an enormous sense of pride, particularly in their home town of Liverpool. The Beatles always made it clear where they came from and that they were proud of their background; this contrasts with Bob Dylan, who did little to acknowledge his origins. Without a shadow of doubt and without being on the city's payroll, the Beatles have been the best tourism officers the city has ever had. Compare this, too, with Buddy Holly. In the 1950s, his home city of Lubbock was a lifeless American city, like many others in the south, and one that would stifle creativity. With a slightly different genetic make-up, Holly would have been content to spend his life in the family tiling business. There was nothing in Lubbock to turn him on, but when he heard early rock'n'roll and black rhythm and blues on the radio, he knew what he wanted to do with his life. Lubbock now attracts tourists but, outside of a statue and the Buddy Holly Center, there is little for them to see. That is not the case in Liverpool: the Beatles may bring tourists to the city, but the city is doing its best to find other attractions to make them stay longer or return.

Liverpool culture on a national stage

In the 1950s, Liverpool was a prosperous port but it had suffered considerable damage in the Second World War. At this time there were still undeveloped bomb-sites in the city and the buildings, to my childhood eyes, seemed dark and depressing. Lime Street station, the key terminus in the city, was covered in soot and nauseating. Although 'Eleanor Rigby' was not specifically about Liverpool, the critic George Melly saw the song as precisely that, a composition that came out of the Beatles' experiences:

> Liverpool was always in their songs but this was about the kind of old woman that I remembered from my childhood and later, very respectable Liverpool women living in two-up, two-down streets with the doorsteps meticulously holystoned, and the church the one solid thing in their lives.... I first heard it at a smart party in London. Someone put it on, and I could see Park Road or Mill Street and those houses going down to the river and I could imagine Eleanor Rigby living in one. It was a complete portrait, a thumbnail sketch that was as solid as a Rembrandt drawing. (Quoted in Leigh 1991: 45–46)

In the early 1960s Liverpool was still the busiest port in the UK and, although the dockers were noted for industrial unease, it was also regarded as one of the friendliest cities in the country. The wit was everywhere. No matter how depressed its economy has been, the city has always generated warmth. To illustrate the point, the Cavern DJ Bob Wooler said that Liverpool was a city of one-liners and ocean liners. This propensity to wit and humour as part of a Liverpudlian identity had already made an impact within British popular culture before the success of the Beatles. There was a long line of Liverpool comics, from the *fin de siècle* music hall entertainer Dan Leno (who spent much of his childhood in the city) through to radio stars such as Robb Wilton, Tommy Handley and Arthur Askey. The cartoonist Norman Thelwell was at the Liverpool College of Art during the war years, almost twenty years before John Lennon. Thus, the idea of Liverpool as a humorous and free-spirited city already had common currency in the national consciousness, an impression that the area's numerous successful entertainers have been keen to propagate. Ken Dodd, for example, calls the area 'Mirthyside' and said:

> We have the soil that talent can grow in. Liverpool people encourage talent and that's why the best comedians, the best entertainers and the best football teams come from Merseyside. Liverpool is a tremendously exuberant city. There's a great life-force here with no respect for dignity. Ask a Merseysider what his favourite subject was at school

and he'll say, 'Playtime'. One reason is that Liverpool's always been a very cosmopolitan city. There's an ethnic mixture of Welsh, Irish and Scots, as well as the English. We had a Chinese quarter before San Francisco. (Quoted in Leigh 1984: 21)

This already established facet of Liverpool identity, then, made the 'Liverpudlian' elements of the Beatles' public persona, interviews and music accessible and understandable to a wider British audience. There is humour throughout the Beatles' recordings and John Lennon sang 'Polythene Pam' in a cod scouse accent in a song which also mocks their own 'yeah, yeah, yeah'. The best-known joke at a Royal Variety Performance wasn't made by a comedian: it was John Lennon telling the audience to rattle their jewelry.

The Beatles as Liverpool ambassadors

The Beatles first made the charts with 'Love Me Do' at the end of 1962 and one huge hit followed another throughout 1963. Right from the start, the Beatles were seen as perfect interviewees and they always talked up Liverpool. In February 1964, at their first American press conference, when the Beatles were asked 'Can you explain your strange English accents?', George Harrison replied 'It's not English. It's Liverpudlian.' By promoting Liverpool, the Beatles were beneficial to the local acts which followed in their wake, as it created a regional identity, and the term 'Merseybeat', as well as 'Beatlemania', entered the language. There was a buzz in the city as one group followed another into the top ten. Did the citizens of Memphis feel this good when Elvis first made it? I doubt it. As it happens, Elvis Presley was the only American to have a number one hit in Britain in 1963 and for thirty-four weeks that year the top-selling record came from Liverpool. Gerry and the Pacemakers, Billy J. Kramer, Cilla Black and the Fourmost were all managed by Brian Epstein, and there were also the Searchers, the Swinging Blue Jeans, the Merseybeats and the Undertakers, who all came to wish they had been managed by Epstein. Curiously, Gerry Marsden (of the Pacemakers) was in two minds about it: he respected Epstein's ability but at the same time realized he was not, and could never be, Epstein's priority.

However, the Beatles were not the first to be ambassadors for Liverpool. Stars of the 1950s like Lita Roza, Frankie Vaughan,

Michael Holliday and Russ Hamilton were proud of their association with the city, and Frankie Vaughan used his fame to promote Boys' Clubs, notably in and around Scotland Road. However, despite crediting the city, these performers would not have brought tourists to Liverpool. Billy Fury might have encouraged a few female fans who wanted to see where his parents lived, but his relationship with the city is more ambivalent. Like the Beatles, he had a poor scholastic record and he spoke with a marked scouse accent, which made him reluctant to talk on stage. How misguided can you be? Zoom ahead a couple of years and you've got the Beatles. As music critic and commentator Paul Du Noyer has observed, 'In 1963 the Beatles' accent and presumed attitudes fed a universal conception of Liverpool as young, fresh, cheeky and optimistic' (Du Noyer 2007: 239). In 1962, the Vernons Girls used their accent for self-mockery on the top twenty single 'You Know What I Mean'. When Billy J. Kramer was interviewed by the UK music paper *Melody Maker* in late 1963, the reporter said that he spoke slowly and softly, as if trying to disguise his Liverpool accent (Roberts 1963).

The Beatles' success was received in a variety of ways in the city, and responses were not always positive. After receiving a telegram from Brian Epstein that the Beatles had reached the top of the charts with their second single, 'Please Please Me', Bob Wooler informed the audience at the Cavern that night. Rather than cheering, the response was muted. Wooler was puzzled but came to realize that the Cavernites had recognized that they would be losing their group. Indeed they were. It wasn't long before Epstein moved his operations to London and the individual Beatles lived in, or moved close to, the capital. They had no choice: there were no recording studios to speak of in Liverpool and the majority of television and radio programmes were made in London. What else could they do? Nonetheless, many Liverpudlians held it against them. Time and again during the 1960s I heard people say 'They've deserted the city'. I still hear it now. To me, it didn't matter: surely being born here was enough and, besides, they took Liverpool with them wherever they went.

The Beatles were brilliant ambassadors for Liverpool but the 'four lads who shook the world' failed to move some influential Merseysiders. When Howard Channon wrote his lengthy *Portrait of Liverpool* in 1970, he included just two passing references to the Beatles and one more to the Cavern. His attitude was shared by the city fathers, who were reluctant to praise the group, and, indeed, my own father, who thought, like many of his generation, that they were a disgrace to the city. Although the Beatles had an incredible welcome home and civic reception through the streets of Liverpool in 1964, the local newspapers revealed that many councillors and residents were uneasy about this and concerned about the cost to the taxpayer. The mixing of politics and celebrity was something new.[1] Liverpool's Labour councillors in the 1960s were highly critical of the Beatles' lifestyle: oh, if only the local folk band the Spinners had had such international success instead. It wasn't until as late as 1984 that the Beatles were given the freedom of the city, which, with a curious similarity to *A Hard Day's Night* in 1964, was twinned with Paul McCartney's charity premiere for his film *Give My Regards to Broad Street*. Fortuitously, the officials then in charge of the city had grown up in the Beatles era or later and appreciated their worth.

The autobiography of the Liverpool MP Eric Heffer, *Never a Yes Man*, indicates his generation's lack of interest in the Beatles, while, at the same time, he appreciated their vote-catching potential. He wrote of the 1964 election:

> There is no doubt in my mind that the astounding Merseybeat boom had a big effect on the outcome of the general election. The groups were young, vibrant, and new. They were in tune with the desires of the people. They asserted working-class values, they looked to the future. I believe the Beatles made a powerful contribution to Labour's victory without recognising it. (Heffer 1991: 107)

But they *did* recognize it. On the eve of the election, Brian Epstein sent the Labour leader, Harold Wilson, a telegram that said 'Hope your group is as much a success as mine'.

Liverpool and tourism

Liverpool at this point was not on the tourist map. Few people came to Liverpool in the early 1960s, hence the small number of hotels and restaurants. The main annual attraction was the Grand National, but in 1961/62 there was the Grand Prix, also at Aintree. The track that was used has now been redeployed, so this is one event that will not return to the city. Alongside music, football was to make the city famous. By a remarkable coincidence, two great managers paraded their strengths at the same time. Liverpool FC was in the Second Division and, in 1959, was humiliated by losing to a non-league side, Worcester City, in the third round of the FA Cup. The *Worcester Evening Times* reportedly said that the players were as 'nervous as old ladies on icy pavements'. A new manager, Bill Shankly, was hired who, like Epstein, knew instinctively about motivation. He recruited Scottish players but he encouraged local ones too and by 1963 the side was doing well. Liverpool won the FA Cup for the first time in its history in 1965. Everton FC was already a good team but was not used to winning. It improved gradually under Harry Catterick, the manager throughout the 1960s, and, as it wanted to be the best team in the city, the improvement in Liverpool FC rubbed off. Everton won the league in 1963 and the FA Cup three years later. The success of Liverpool and Everton, when coupled with Merseybeat, improved the city's image. Individually, the Beatles themselves took little interest in football, but Gerry and the Pacemakers' song 'You'll Never Walk Alone' was taken up by the Kop choir. The so-called escape routes for working-class adolescents (football and music) were said to be what saved Liverpool from falling into decline.

In the 1960s, the population of Liverpool and its suburbs was around a million, and the general impression, erroneous as it happens, was that the city was downtrodden. Around 20 per cent of the workforce was engaged on the docks and employment was readily available in the early 1960s. Many Merseybeat musicians had no qualms about leaving a job, as they were certain that they would find another when they wanted one. Both Ford and Triumph had factories in Liverpool, although Triumph didn't last long and Ford's, along with the dockers, gave Liverpool its reputation for industrial unrest.

The Beatles emerged at a time when there was an appetite and a marketplace for teenage leisure pursuits. In the 1950s, everybody had seemed old – at the earliest opportunity, youngsters dressed like their parents. That there was nothing for teenagers is illustrated by the BBC's television broadcasting hours. There was a children's hour in the late afternoon and then the station shut down until the adult programmes began at 7 p.m. The mould was broken with a show aimed specifically at teenagers, *Six-Five Special*, in 1957. 'It was possibly the best-ever time to be a teenager', said Marty Wilde, one of the UK's first rock'n'roll stars:

We had money; we had jobs; there were no drugs; conscription was abolished, and we could enjoy ourselves at coffee-bars without wanting to drink. Most of all, we had the music. The music of the late '50s and early '60s was so original and so wonderful. (Quoted in Leigh 2004: 6)

However, the music that was then on offer largely originated in America. Marty Wilde's hit records were often covers of American hits, while Cliff Richard and Tommy Steele were intent on becoming family entertainers. Billy Fury's album *The Sound of Fury* (1960) was up to the standard of Sun Records in Memphis, but he changed direction for a career of well performed but somewhat uninspiring beat ballads. Johnny Kidd and the Pirates made two splendid records, 'Please Don't Touch' (1959) and 'Shakin' All Over' (1960), but by the time of the Merseybeat explosion Kidd seemed too old.

This period was evocatively captured in the film *Nowhere Boy* (2009), directed by Sam Taylor-Wood. John Lennon's adolescence is beautifully portrayed and the relationships with his absentee mother, Julia, and his aunt, Mimi, appear both accurate and fair. Most of all, you can sense John's affection for the new music. There is no evidence for what John thought of Screamin' Jay Hawkins' 'I Put a Spell on You', but this song conveys Lennon's passion for rock'n'roll as well as his relationship with his newly found mother. *Nowhere Boy* presents a wonderfully positive picture of Liverpool that it is sure to bring more tourists to the city.

Liverpool and the United States

There is a scene in *Nowhere Boy* where John Lennon is given some American rhythm and blues records by a merchant seaman, a so-called 'Cunard Yank'. However, I am unconvinced about the importance of Cunard Yanks in the Beatles' story. Brian Epstein's superbly stocked record shop, NEMS, was surely more significant and, indeed, is one of the luckiest factors in the Beatles' story. Much has been made of the influence of the Cunard Yanks on Merseybeat, but there is no evidence that they brought in rare rock'n'roll records from America. Believe me, I have tried my best to find it. The Beatles never acknowledged the Cunard Yanks. Although Liverpool groups recorded over 350 American covers, every one of the originals had been released in the UK. Those originals may not have sold well, but the NEMS record shop in Whitechapel stocked every release, as it was Epstein's belief that no customer should leave the shop dissatisfied. Back then, customers could listen to potential purchases in listening booths, which explains why some cover versions have wrong words or omit verses: the musicians hadn't been able to write down the words quickly enough.

Back in the 1930s, the Musicians' Union had banned American artists from performing in the UK. It was thought that if, say, Louis Armstrong were to tour the UK, British musicians would be deprived of work. The American Federation of Musicians took a similar stand, but there were few British musicians the American public wanted to see. Another lucky factor in the Beatles' story is that this long-running dispute was resolved in the 1950s and the Beatles were able to play in America without union problems. Before the Beatles, Cliff Richard made a half-hearted attempt to establish himself in America, but he was not prepared to put in the effort after he found himself near the bottom of a bill on a US package tour. By very early 1963, the four members of the Beatles were individually known in the UK and people were asking each other, 'Who's your favourite Beatle?' In February 1964, they appeared on *The Ed Sullivan Show* and conquered the United States. Surprisingly, a caption for John Lennon played across the screen during the show stated that he was married, but the fact that he was a father was either not known or not revealed.

When asked what they thought of the Beatles' success at the time, several Liverpool musicians felt that they had been lucky. That could be jealousy but the Beatles' undeniably catchy songs could have been played competently, but not written, by several of the other Liverpool bands. Or could they? The Beatles ticked all the boxes – good songs, good playing, good looks and *joie de vivre*. Kingsize Taylor may be right when he says his band, the Dominoes, was technically as good as the Beatles in 1963, but he resembled a bouncer, and that was that. For a measure of who was photogenic and who wasn't, look at Astrid Kirchherr's collection (Kirchherr and Scheler 1995): she met all the Liverpool musicians who came to Germany but she photographed only the good-lookers. And another thing about the Beatles is that they *always* looked cool. No matter what they wore, they still looked great, even in ridiculous bathing costumes. This is not the case with other bands – look at the Kinks in their hunting jackets, the Rolling Stones dressed psychedelically, or the Bee Gees in almost anything.

If the Beatles had a philosophy, it was this: they wanted to be a part of whatever was happening. This can be seen over and over again in their work and their behaviour. For example, studio technology was advancing all the time during the 1960s and the Beatles were there with every change. In 1963 they would rehearse their material beforehand and then record a song in an hour. By 1967, they were effectively living in the studio and writing as they went along. They had the confidence to play other instruments and as soon as they had learnt something, they would write new songs. When Donovan showed Paul McCartney his chording technique, Paul wrote 'Blackbird'. This ability to learn new techniques and bring them into their music was no small achievement. In 1962, the DJs were playing Craig Douglas records and in 1967 Jimi Hendrix. The Liverpool bands were floundering by then and only the Beatles did well in the psychedelic era. I have never understood, though, why they didn't join the blues-based London culture. Their 1968 track 'Yer Blues' shows how easily they could have done that.

The Beatles and remembrances of Liverpool

Although the media regard the Beatles as a Liverpool group (which is true), they don't sound like a Liverpool group on most of their recordings. Most of the time they were doing their best to sound American, and by the mid-1960s they had become a London group. Not for nothing did they call an album *Abbey Road*. Many songs have been written about Liverpool, most of them folk based and most of them written after the Second World War. They include 'Liverpool Lullaby', 'The Leaving of Liverpool' and 'Liverpool Lou', a song that Paul McCartney was to produce for Scaffold. Despite writing so personally, John Lennon rarely wrote specifically about Liverpool, although his original lyric for 'In My Life' is packed with local references, viewed on a bus ride to the city centre. The Beatles' specific portrayal of their childhood surroundings came with the double-A-sided single that featured the songs 'Penny Lane' and 'Strawberry Fields Forever', released early in 1967. This magnificent 45 combined McCartney's surreal and idyllic vision of 'Penny Lane' with Lennon's drugged-out reminiscences of his childhood visits to the Salvation Army Home 'Strawberry Fields', close to his house on

Menlove Avenue. Spurred on by the success of these compositions, it is said that Lennon and McCartney did consider writing a whole album called 'Liverpool', but soon dropped the idea in favour of *Sgt. Pepper's Lonely Hearts Club Band*.

John Lennon scrutinized his roots in a very different way in 'Working Class Hero' (1970). Lennon was an inspired but slapdash lyricist, generally far sharper than McCartney, and his views were inconsistent and his reflections contradictory. Following sessions with the psychologist Arthur Janov, he explored his childhood in this bitter and defiant song. The lyric is full of ambiguities and it is not clear whether he regarded himself as working class or whether he wanted to be a hero of the working classes, or both. In an interview with the radical magazine *Red Mole* in 1971, Lennon said that he had been 'brought up to hate and fear the police as a natural enemy', but he was surely posturing. I'm sure Aunt Mimi never told him that. But the song was prescient. From the late 1960s, like many northern cities, Liverpool was battered, socially, economically and politically, and was often cited as the centre of the black economy. Manchester life was depicted more warmly in popular culture, for example in the long-running soap opera *Coronation Street*. In the 1970s, economic and political troubles brought Liverpool unwelcome publicity. The riots in 1981 around Liverpool 8 (Toxteth) focused attention on inner-city deprivation. In the mid-1980s the city symbolized the threat posed to the Labour party, and indeed the country, by Militant. To the outsider, Liverpool was seen as a working-class city full of troublemakers.

In recent years the image of Liverpool has changed and the remaining members of the Beatles have engaged with the city in different ways. In 1991, Paul McCartney, with the assistance of the conductor Carl Davis, wrote *Liverpool Oratorio*, a homage to his roots, which was premiered at Liverpool Cathedral. We were led to believe that this was an important classical work, telling the story of Shanty, who was born during an air raid in 1942. Its premise, taken from Liverpool Institute's credo, was that wherever you are born, you have responsibilities to your roots, and McCartney has lived up to that. The DVD release contains a tour of the old Liverpool Institute building by McCartney and some personal reminiscences in a song called 'Liverpool'. McCartney had the vision to change the derelict Liverpool Institute building into an academy for Performing

Arts, a *Fame* school, if you like. There was so little development in Liverpool at the time that this was a brave move. LIPA, to use its familiar acronym, opened in 1996 and is now world famous, not just for its link with McCartney but for the excellence of its teaching and the quality of its graduates. Flip through any theatre programme and you'll find CVs that credit LIPA. Paul McCartney was always the Beatle who was most attached to, and attracted by, the city. He still has a house on the Wirral and he returns for family reunions and songwriting seminars and graduation ceremonies at LIPA. Every time McCartney tours or introduces a new work (a book of poems, *Liverpool Oratorio*), he includes Liverpool in his schedule. I did, however, think that his contribution to the Capital of Culture was lame: he gave a great concert at Anfield, to be sure, but, heck, giving great concerts is what he does all the time.

While McCartney's relationship with the city is at an all-time high, Ringo Starr's relationship is in doubt. He was the much-heralded special guest at the opening of the Capital of Culture celebrations. They went well and, fortunately, nobody noticed that he was miming the drums on the roof of St George's Hall (for logistical reasons, he had no choice). He was cheered at the opening concert of the ECHO Arena when he said that he was close to returning to the city. A few days later he appeared on BBC1's *Friday Night with Jonathan Ross*. The presenter for once wasn't encouraging his guest to be outrageous. He asked a simple question about Liverpool, thereby enabling Ringo to plug the celebrations. Only he didn't. He claimed that he had felt obliged to praise the city. It transpired that, although he waived his fee for the Liverpool event, he had run up astronomical expenses. Ringo didn't apologize for his outburst and he may have meant it. His remark in some way mirrors John Lennon's comment in a *Rolling Stone* interview in 1971: 'America is where it's at.... I regret profoundly that I was not an American and not born in Greenwich Village' (quoted in Wenner 1971). As far as I know, Lennon did not repeat this remark and I doubt if he believed it: after all, he had a trunk marked 'Liverpool' in his flat in the Dakota building in New York. But how should we evaluate Ringo's comment? What attractions does Liverpool hold for a jet-setter who lives in Monte Carlo? In 1992, when Ringo made a documentary for the Disney channel, he walked around Liverpool and it was evident that he had had a sad childhood, in and out of hospitals. His view of the city may therefore be jaundiced. However, I prefer to think of his remark to Ross as a joke that went wrong. When Ringo returned from India before the other Beatles, he commented that the Maharishi's enclave was 'like Butlin's'. His remark in 2008 was equally flippant, only this time it wasn't funny, particularly as the city was striving hard for success. Radio phone-ins were full of listeners who had no time for the former Beatle. His new album, stocked up at Zavvi in Clayton Square, was relegated to the sale rack. Oddly, its lead track, 'Liverpool 8', was an affectionate, if cliché-ridden, look at the city. At least he hadn't revived 'We Gotta Get Out of This Place'.

From time to time, comparisons link Liverpool to New Orleans. Both cities are ports and both cities have shameful pasts through the slave trade, but both cities are now cosmopolitan. Jazz began in New Orleans in 1895 and Merseybeat in Liverpool in 1962. The world's most successful jazz musician, Louis Armstrong, came from New Orleans and the world's most successful songwriters, Lennon and McCartney, came from Liverpool. There is one major difference: one city was embracing jazz and the other rejecting it. In 2001, both New Orleans and Liverpool renamed their airports after one of their musical sons – namely, Louis Armstrong and John Lennon. It is not yet possible to fly direct from Louis Armstrong to John Lennon or vice versa, but the time may come.

The Capital of Culture celebrations proved to be highly successful but the city has now been hit by the credit crunch like everywhere else, and who knows what the future will hold. Certainly tourism will be hit, but it will be tourism that brings the city through again, and I am sure that pilgrimages to the Beatles' home will contribute to the recovery. So much of Liverpool now says 'Beatles'. Tourists can visit the Beatles Story and John and Paul's National Trust childhood homes, gaze at the achievements of the band on the 'Wall of Hits' outside the Cavern, look at Beatles artifacts and images in *The Beat Goes On* exhibition at World Museum Liverpool, and purchase memorabilia in the Beatles Shop. In 2008 the Hard Days Night Hotel opened and the first 'Beatles Day' was launched on 10 July, with plans for it to become an annual event. Each year also a Beatle convention is held over the August bank holiday weekend which includes the presence of musicians, promoters and friends, often from Liverpool, who were associated with the Beatles. Through mortality and illness, there is a dwindling number of personalities to invite as, by now, anyone who saw the Beatles at the Cavern has to be a senior citizen. Given ten years, the guest list will have a distinctly second-hand feel: we will have tribute speakers as well as tribute acts. Some sites, such as the building which housed NEMS in Whitechapel, are not recognized, however. The Beatles' global success has transformed Liverpool into 'Music City, UK' and many have argued about whether this is good or bad for emerging musicians. Certainly in the 1970s, it was regarded as a negative, but now it has to be an advantage. I suspect the musicians who feel constrained by the Beatles' presence are the ones who don't have much talent in the first place. There were plenty of musicians in the 1960s who, rather than being inhibited by the Beatles' talent, used it as a springboard for something new.

Conclusion

In this chapter, I have refrained from calling Liverpool 'the fifth Beatle'. This is woolly-headed thinking, akin to the *Liverpool Echo* listing Red Rum among the top ten Liverpudlians. Bill Heckle, the joint owner of the Cavern, said:

> There were so many elements of the Beatles that were typically Liverpool: you could put them 20 or 25 miles away in Wigan or Widnes and they would not have been the Beatles. Liverpool, I am certain, had a huge input in making the Beatles. (Quoted in Leigh 2004: 10)

There is a street sign at the entrance to the city: 'Welcome to Liverpool, Home of the Beatles'. This is akin to Warwickshire's view of Shakespeare. When Jefferson Starship played the Cavern in 2004, Paul Kantner put it more prosaically: he looked round the room and said to the audience, 'So this is where western civilization got fucked up'. No doubt about it, a working-class city is some place to be. Let's not sing 'The Leaving of Liverpool' anymore: let's appreciate the leading of Liverpool.

Note

1   The Lord Mayor's files about the Beatles' homecoming can be viewed at the Liverpool Record Office.

References

Channon, Howard (1970) *Portrait of Liverpool*. London: Hale.

Du Noyer, Paul (2007) 'Subversive Dreamers: Liverpool Songwriting from the Beatles to the Zutons'. In: Deryn Rees-Jones and Michael Murphy (eds) *Writing Liverpool: Essays and Interviews*. Liverpool: Liverpool University Press. pp. 239–51.

Heffer, Eric (1991) *Never A Yes Man*. London: Verso.

Kirchherr, Astrid and Max Scheler (1995) *Liverpool Days: The Photographs of Max Scheler and Astrid Kirchherr*. Guildford: Genesis.

Leigh, Spencer (1984) *Let's Go Down the Cavern*. London: Vermilion.

Leigh, Spencer (1991) *Speaking Words of Wisdom: Reflections on the Beatles*, Liverpool: Cavern City Tours.

Leigh, Spencer (2004) *Twist and Shout: Merseybeat, the Cavern, the Star-Club and the Beatles*. Liverpool: Nirvana.

Roberts, Chris (1963) 'Billy J. Kramer'. *Melody Maker*, 30 November.

Wenner, Jann S. (1971) 'The Rolling Stone Interview: John Lennon, Part II'. *Rolling Stone*, 4 February, issue 75. pp. 17–29.

CHAPTER 3

From sea shanties to cosmic scousers: the city, memory and representation in Liverpool's popular music

Robert Strachan

'Magical Liverpool'

It was the mid-1990s and I was about to move cities to undertake postgraduate study on popular music at the University of Liverpool. On telling a friend the news he momentarily went misty eyed and sighed 'Ah, magical Liverpool'. Despite my real experience of the city being confined to a couple of hours at Anfield football ground sometime in the early 1980s I kind of knew what he meant. The same friend had introduced me to the *Sgt. Pepper's Lonely Hearts Club* album some years earlier. We had listened to the record in its entirety in his north London flat after a night out clubbing. As fans of both pop and electronic dance music we marvelled at its inventive use of production techniques and the way in which it wove classic songwriting into a strange psychedelic sound-world. However, this was by no means my first experience of the Beatles. In 1970s Leeds, my long-haired primary school teacher had spent the entirety of our music lessons teaching us to sing 'Yellow Submarine', 'Penny Lane' and the Scaffold's 'Lily the Pink'. This Beatles-orientated strain in my education continued into secondary school, where my physical education teacher organized Beatles-themed school concerts and showed us videos of Beatles documentaries and the *Yellow Submarine*[1] film in those fun end-of-term sessions before Christmas.

By the time I arrived in Liverpool I had already accumulated a store of associations and expectations. I had read books and films about the Beatles, been a fan of Liverpool bands such as Echo and the Bunnymen and Teardrop Explodes, as well as having been exposed to news and media representations of contemporary Liverpool in dramas such as *Boys from the Blackstuff*,[2] *No Surrender*[3] and countless others. My experiences of living in the city were thus refracted through what I already 'knew' about it. Being a music fan, however, it was the representation of the city through music that remained powerful for me. Aside from being an *aide memoire* in my own personal memory, music had constructed a mythical version of place that I took with me, colouring my expectations of the city. In essence, my understanding of a 'magical' Liverpool tapped into a wider collective memory about the city, transmitted through particular cultural representations.

Collective memory

This chapter examines how representations of the city in music and Liverpool's musical cultures contribute to the construction of collective memory. It examines two main aspects of the way in which images and discourses about Liverpool as a city are transmitted through music. On the one hand, it explores how the music, lyrics, image and aesthetic agenda of the performers of popular music are bound up with particular representations of place. On the other, it examines how media accounts and critical representations often contextualize the city's music and its prominent performers in very specific ways. It argues that these factors combine to constantly reinforce a cultural legacy that is at the heart of collective memory. It begins by tracing representations of Liverpool in song through the folk revivals of the nineteenth and twentieth centuries, and goes on to examine how the phenomenal success of the Beatles served to cement particular representations of the city in the national and international consciousness, before it examines specific moments of representation from the 1980s to the 2000s.

The concept of collective memory has been used by cultural historians to conceptualize not only the memories of people who have lived through particular experiences, but also 'the representation of the past and the making of it into a shared cultural knowledge … in "vehicles of memory" such as books, films, museums, commemorations and others' (Confino 1997: 1386). Both of these elements have been understood as active within a collective memory, through which social groups derive an awareness of their unity (Asserman 1995). Here, an 'objectivized culture' serves to preserve the store of memory relating to a particular group and leads to the 'concretion of identity' for that group (Asserman 1995: 130). As a predominant medium of the twentieth century, recorded popular music has been seen as a powerful transmitter of collective memory and a way of connecting an individual's sense of self to a broader community (Lipsitz 1990; Van Dijck 2006; Strachan 2009).

Popular music and collective memory

Specific conceptualizations of Liverpool's identity are, of course, firmly rooted in the material conditions of the city. For 150 years it was a centre for international exchange, fostering a cultural connection across the Atlantic towards North America, while at the same time upholding a distinct local identity within the UK. Added to this, throughout the twentieth century the city experienced a series of economic slumps far more severe than those experienced by any other British city. From the late 1960s, the decline of Liverpool's port led to massive disinvestment from the city and dereliction on a tragic scale. From this time the economic base of sea trade, shipping, ship building and insurance all but disappeared, leading to sharp economic decline, outward migration and high levels of unemployment, with significant areas of the city centre associated with this primary industry falling into disrepair. Belcham (2000: 63) notes that this particular set of historical sensibilities has led to a 'scouse cosmopolitanism' linked with an 'otherness' to the rest of the UK which has defined Liverpool's self-definition and self-representation.

This chapter seeks to examine how, throughout the second half of the twentieth century, Liverpool's musical cultures consistently represented, engaged with and articulated city history in a number of ways. In particular, it examines the duality of celebration and loss articulated through popular song. Different tropes of expression are identifiable in the lyrics and music of many local music makers. These include: pride in local culture as a cultural response to economic decline and an identity which is seen as under threat; nostalgic responses, often resulting in sentimental representations of the city's culture; and celebratory responses to post-industrial decline and the particular cultures spawned by unemployment. Musicians also frequently mine the very specific musical culture related to the city's past as a seaport and thus align themselves with a particular lineage of influential musicians within the city. The past is often present within these representations, as Liverpool's maritime history, industrial decline, unemployment and 'dole culture' are frequently evoked. It is, of course, not only through song that these narratives about the city and its attendant identities are produced and circulated. However, this chapter focuses on the prominent ways in which existing constructions of the city, identifiable in social discourse and the wider media, are animated by musicians.

Liverpool and the folk revivals

Part of this strain of representation can be related to the construction of a folk authenticity engendered by successive folk revivals. As Middleton (1990: 127) notes, folk music has been seen by its protagonists as 'an authentic expression of a way of life now past or about to disappear' and has tended to draw upon narratives related to the rural (and later urban) working classes. Liverpool's position as the most prominent UK seaport of the nineteenth century meant that many tunes and songs related to the city fitted with these overriding thematic concerns. Accordingly, a wealth of Liverpool-related material can be found within the folk repertoire. Traditional songs such as 'Johnny Todd' and 'The Leaving of Liverpool', along with countless shanties, ballads and hornpipes, form part of a body of work which emerged through collectors of the late nineteenth and early twentieth century who sought to preserve the oral tradition. 'The Liverpool Hornpipe', for instance, was collected by the Chicago police chief Francis O'Neill and published in his defining 1907 collection *The Dance Music of Ireland*. This hornpipe was also recorded by the great Sligo/New York fiddle player Michael Coleman, one of the first traditional Irish musicians to have a successful recording career. Similarly 'The Leaving of Liverpool', first published in *Songs of the Sailor and Lumberman*, by William Main Doerflinger (1951), a maritime song collector, was taken from a bosun on the *General Cox*, who had apparently learned the song in the 1880s. The song went on to be a staple of the second folk revival, of the 1950s and 1960s, was adopted as part of the repertoire of the Dubliners and Ewan MacColl and was adapted by a young Bob Dylan as 'Farewell'. Liverpool's maritime heritage was also mined on the 1958 Topic Records' release of Stan Kelly's *Liverpool Packet* (recorded with Leon Rosselson and Geoff Rose), a collection of Liverpool seafaring songs. This concept was later revisited by Ross MacManus, Elvis Costello's father, in 1972 on his Rediffusion album *The Leaving of Liverpool*.

The second folk revival also saw the city being used as subject matter for a new generation of songwriters who were drawing upon folk idioms in their work. Writers such as Stan Kelly, Dominic Behan and Pete McGovern were less concerned with the maritime tradition as with the experiences of Liverpool's urban working class and the communication of a sense of pride and triumph in the face of adversity. Stan Kelly's 'Liverpool Lullaby' for example, tells of a 'mucky kid' with an abusive alcoholic father whose mother dreams of 'better days' in a retreat to the suburbs (Knotty Ash) by winning the Littlewoods pools. Similarly, McGovern's 'In My Liverpool Home' (brought to wider attention by the Spinners and the Scaffold) characterizes the city as one of poverty, violence and 'hard knocks'.

These representations of Liverpool fit with wider discursive folk formations common within the international folk revival. First, they are part of a social realism that chimed with the political discourses of the movement. As Brocken (2003: 20) notes, folk song in the UK became 'a vehicle ... for those interested in the rediscovery of working class art' in reaction to consumerism, Americanization and mass culture. Secondly, connections to place (in terms of regional singing or playing styles) and representations of place form key parts of folk authenticity (see for example Sommers Smith 1998). Within the folk context, the preservation of local difference became increasingly important, given folk's dialectic with a mass culture which was perceived as inauthentic and homogenizing. These representations also have broader implications relating to music's place in the construction of community. As Cohen (2003: 185) notes, music is active in 'stimulating collective memory' by providing a 'sense of identity, belonging and place' and by helping to develop, define and distinguish a particular community *as* a community, 'often in situations of considerable uncertainty'. In other words, we can see these folk representations as active in reinforcing and concretizing particular narratives of place and history, along with a sense of otherness, within Liverpool identity. This substantial body of work thus provides a powerful cultural legacy within the city's music history. As Du Noyer (2007: 241) notes, 'they are a long standing characteristic of Liverpool; they've informed its cultural atmosphere, and no local songwriter has ever grown up in ignorance of this tradition'.

Folk repertoire and popular culture

It is important to note that these folk representations seeped into a wider popular culture at both a local and a national level. There was a local popularization of folk music itself through the Spinners' populist take on folk material and through the widespread appeal of a BBC Radio Merseyside show run by Jacqueline McDonald (of the folk group Jacqui and Bridie). However, there was also an appropriation of folk material by musicians from differing musical backgrounds. Brocken (2010: 174–75) points to the 'mingling of folk and local popular traditions' by local artists within the city's live music and working men's club circuits. He notes that country and cabaret artists would often include comedic or nostalgic 'folk-style' material in their routines, which gave them 'far greater levels of local popularity', by tapping into 'a search for a more personal tradition via remembrances of idealized childhoods and nostalgia for long-dead relatives and work patterns' (2010: 175). Similarly, in the 1960s and 1970s the folk repertoire began to be covered by Liverpool recording artists, resulting in something of a shift in musical register. In the hands of artists such as Cilla Black and the Scaffold, folk authenticity was transformed into a popular sentimentality, which fed back into the collective folk memory of the city's past.

Folk songs about the city attained national prominence by being re-recorded by pop singers, both from the city itself and from elsewhere. For example 'Liverpool Lullaby' was included on the 1966 album *In My Life* by US folk singer Judy Collins. Collins' version is delivered in her signature style, the purity of her vocal delivery backed with a sensitive and stripped down arrangement of finger-picked guitar and concertina. In the context of a set by one of the leading figures of the folk revival, the song can be seen as in keeping with the recording conventions of folk artists of the time.[4] Generally, albums would consist of material drawn from the traditional (often across geographical locations) along with newer material within various folk idioms. Collins' version is in stark contrast to the 1969 recording of the song by Cilla Black. Black's version is given a lush orchestration by George Martin, placing the recording within a sound-world more akin to mainstream British pop contemporaries such as Dusty Springfield and Petula Clark or the US pop of Burt Bacharach and Hal David. The specific musical setting of the recording serves to distance the text from the folk tradition and to place it within the emotional range and expressive traditions of pop. In addition, the lyrics are delivered in an accentuated 'scouse' accent, with the use of Liverpool diminutives such as la' and da' (for lad and dad) further inscribing the recording with a sense of local specificity. What in the hands of Collins could be understood as a universal social commentary upon the insidious effects of poverty becomes recoded as a very specific representation of locality.

Black's 'Liverpool Lullaby' was part of a wider trend among Liverpool pop artists to appropriate Liverpool folk material. When moved out of the folk idiom, the 'localness' of the material becomes more apparent. Furthermore, the exaggeration of the characteristics of accent found in Black's recording was a prime strategy in this wider recoding of the material as primarily local. For example, the Scaffold's version of 'In My Liverpool Home' (delivered as 'in me Liverpool 'ome') and Dominic Behan's 'Liverpool Lou' were both sung in exaggerated 'scouse' accents. Likewise, the Beatles' version of the nineteenth-century Liverpool street song 'Maggie Mae' sees John Lennon consciously using flattened vowels in a heightened way not found elsewhere in the band's repertoire and deliberately over-exaggerating the word 'Liverpool' to an almost comedic extent. These examples constitute highly performative enactments of localness which connote belonging, particular class formations and particular cultural associations related to 'scouse identity'. Belcham positions scouse as an accent (and a cultural marker) that emerged in the twentieth century as a cultural response to the city's decline (Belcham 2000; see also Honeybone 2007). He notes that the accent became the 'essential medium for the projection and representation of the local micro-culture, the "scouse" blend of truculent defiance, collective solidarity, scallywaggery and fatalist humour which sets Liverpool and its inhabitants apart' (Belcham 2000: 33). Similarly, Bolland, while highlighting that scouseness is the site of heightened and contested discourses relating to identity, nevertheless sees the scouse vernacular as a key factor in the shaping of local identity and difference. He argues that an effective understanding of a scouser is not only spatial but also sonic. Thus the 'sonoric landscape of spoken scouse' (Bolland 2010: 1) is central in patterns of inclusion and exclusion and a key 'cultural symbol of people and place' (2010: 7).

While I am not suggesting that the decision to use scouse inflections in these instances is utterly contrived, the fact that they are used does constitute a conscious creative decision, marking them out at a time when a flattening of accent or the adoption of a 'mid-Atlantic' drawl was the norm in British popular music. Moreover, the use of the scouse accent within these recordings can be seen as a cashing in of a number of cultural associations. By foregrounding this regional accent, the singers created a distinctly working-class feel (despite being delivered by middle-class vocalists such as Lennon and John Gorman of the Scaffold) with associations of unpretentiousness and honesty, along with an affectionate nod to the city's past.[5] This class element was also part of a strain within popular culture in the 1960s which celebrated working-class identity in a time of demographic and social change. However, while the Kinks and the Small Faces used Cockney inflections in their work, other regional accents were not usually detectable in British popular music of the time.[6] The Liverpool accent is notable, then, by its presence. Arguably, these artists were consciously drawing upon pre-existent notions of scouse identity that were widely circulated by nationally successful entertainers from the 1930s onwards (see chapter 2). Moreover, the unprecedented cultural impact of the Beatles carried with it an internationally mediated mythology relating to the city and its music. By the time the Beatles recorded 'Maggie Mae' (in the context of the *Let It Be* album, which deliberately looked towards the band's roots) they could afford to ironically pastiche their geographical heritage without fear of being misunderstood.

The Beatles, suburbia and nostalgia

Consideration of the direct references to the city within the Beatles' recordings reveals a particular nostalgic and primarily suburban strain of representation. Even though it may be more accurate to think of the Beatles' meteoric rise and artistic development as more of a story embedded within the social contexts of mid-1960s London, the group's reliance on Liverpool as a thematic constant within their (later) work, and the wider mediation of Liverpool as a defining influence upon it, clearly cast a shadow over subsequent musicians in the city. This worldwide mediation of Liverpool can be seen to work in complex and ambiguous ways. In fact, it was only after the Beatles moved from the city (fairly early in their career) that they began to directly reflect upon the city in their work. As Daniels (2006: 34) notes, 'the leaving of Liverpool for London, where they were taken up as key figures in the capital's pop pantheon, sharpened a sense of personal memory and literary history in the Beatles' work'. Accordingly, Liverpool became totemic of nostalgia and their representations of the city were generally of a mythical version of a 1950s Liverpool which no longer (and probably never) existed.

For example, early draft versions for the lyrics of the 1965 release 'In My Life' (displayed in *The Beat Goes On* exhibition), while unpublished, give an insight into John Lennon's creative process and an illustration of the way in which both Lennon and McCartney were using Liverpool as inspiration in their songwriting. According to Lennon himself, the song 'started out as a bus journey from my house at 250 Menlove Avenue to town, mentioning all the places I could recall' (Sheff 1981: 110) but was written in his house in Surrey. The landmarks listed in the draft are either those from Lennon's suburban childhood in south Liverpool (Church Road, Calderstones Park, Penny Lane) or city-centre locations which were no longer there (such as a deserted tram-shed and the 'Dockers Umbrella', a colloquial name for the overhead tramline which was demolished in 1958). Despite the fact that Lennon would revise the song to make the lyrics a more general reflection on memory and contemplation (as he considered the list structure of the song aesthetically uninteresting), the draft lyrics are nonetheless an early precursor to what was to follow.

Both 'Penny Lane' and 'Strawberry Fields' (released as a double-A-side single in 1967) echo the nostalgic yearning of 'In My Life' and are firmly rooted in an idyllic and ultimately *suburban* representation of the city. We can read these particular representations of the city suburbs as being rooted in a central component of nostalgia, that is, the desire to return to an idealized past as a way of reconciling the sense of loss and uncertainty engendered by the rapid changes in our social fabric and daily lives endemic to modernity. As Green (2005: 261) notes, the portrait painted by 'Penny Lane' was one of an 'idealized English suburban way of life, safe from the dangers of the city itself, peopled by unthreatening characters who lend a feeling of steady continuity to a place via a sun-drenched series of vignettes of the comfortably familiar characters to be found there'. Taken in isolation there may be a tendency to see such nostalgic representations as backward looking and ultimately regressive. However, such representations of the suburbs must, of course, be placed in a wider musical and cultural context, and it is clear that the Beatles were drawing upon their childhood memories as part of their artistic turn towards a whimsical psychedelic aesthetic. Daniels (2006) sees 'Penny Lane' and 'Strawberry Fields' echo 'In My Life' as part of a wider retrospective, pastoral and ultimately English strain within British popular music from the mid-1960s which utilized images of childhood and country life (shared by bands such as the Kinks and Pink Floyd during the Syd Barrett era). The overall utopian thrust of psychedelia and its position within the emerging counterculture may be framed within the progressive formulation of nostalgia that Pickering and Keightley (2006: 921) identify as signifying the 'desire not to return but to recognize aspects of the past as the basis for renewal and satisfaction in the future'.

Mediation and the cultural legacy of Merseybeat

The evocation of a suburban idyll filtered through the dreamlike musical context of psychedelia described above may seem to be essentially at odds with the dominant media framing of Merseybeat within a gritty urban mythology. However, the two representations are equally powerful in constructing a collective memory of the city through music. As Inglis notes in chapter 1, the grouping together of Merseybeat bands by the music and media industries in the early 1960s was a useful framing device through which to promote and understand a new wave of popular music acts which were emerging contemporaneously. Inglis argues that the concentration on place and locality may have been less to do with the emergence of a particularly localized sound and more to do with a promotional angle, which must be viewed in relation to the hitherto London-dominated UK music industry. Whatever the nuances of the relationship between locality and sound, there is no doubt that the heavy promotion of Liverpool acts in the media carried with it very specific representations of the city to a national and international audience. From an early stage, the context of the city provided a neat 'explanation' for the Merseybeat 'explosion', whereby an assumed set of characteristics relating to Liverpool and its people were given as central reasons for its growth and ultimate success.

The voice-over of *The Beatles' Story*, a documentary album which reached number seven in *Billboard* magazine's US album charts in 1965, is typical of the way in which the Beatles and Merseybeat more generally were framed at the time. A now familiar series of clichés relating to deprivation, faded grandeur and underlying violence is used to place the Beatles in a specific geographical and social context. The voice-over starts with a repeated mantra of 'It started in Liverpool, England', before it goes on to describe the city:

> Liverpool, a poor but proud seaport which took more pride in her history than hope for her future, has lifted her head. Instead of the sombre rattle of poverty echoing faintly from her old cobblestoned streets, sounds which mixed with the sounds of ships' horns and pulsating, organ-like police sirens, there's a new sound of hope.[7]

Similarly, the 1963 television programme *Beat City*[8] (which included live footage of a variety of Merseybeat acts) was introduced with images of deprivation and urban decline. Again, familiar invocations of innovation through hardship and the spirit of Liverpool's people are put forward as explaining the phenomenal success of the city's popular music.

This binding of Merseybeat music to a very specific context of urban decline and deprivation is clearly problematic and various critics have represented the city in ways which can be seen as reductive and downright erroneous (see Cohen 2007: 62). The question of whether these representations are historically 'correct' is perhaps something of a distraction, as it is their repeated use across differing media representations which is significant. Indeed, the Beatles consciously constructed and played with these types of representation throughout their career. Tatom Letts (2008), for example, describes how the animated film *Yellow Submarine* deliberately taps into the Beatles' existing mythology created by the band's history and music by contrasting a drab vision of Liverpool with the psychedelic imaginary of 'Pepperland'. In the second scene of the film, Liverpool is portrayed, in a deliberately limited palette of muted tones of grey, brown and dark green, through images of terraced houses, cobbled streets, graffiti and derelict buildings.

This representational aspect of the Beatles continues to be sustained by the multimillion dollar Beatles industry up to the present day. Apple Corps (the company that handles the band's business affairs) has maintained careful control of the Beatles' music and image in a conscious effort to maintain the band's mystique and economic and cultural value. The company has been very restrictive in terms of licensing the Beatles' music for film and advertising and refuses to let the band's recordings appear on compilations (in a conscious effort to maintain the idea of the band as 'timeless' and apart from their 1960s peers). Significantly, Apple Corps and EMI (the record company that signed the Beatles) have not come to an agreement on digital downloading, despite the economic importance of the digital sales market, and the Beatles remain the last major act not to have their music for release via digital stores. Instead, Apple has been astute in utilizing new formats and differing settings for the band's music since the 1970s, resulting in a series of 'event' releases, including the simultaneous 1973 release of the *Blue Album* and *Red Album* greatest hits collections, carefully managed CD re-releases in 1987, the *Beatles Anthology* VHS set in the 1990s, the 2006 *Love* remix album (with an associated show produced in collaboration with Cirque du Soleil) and the 2009 release of album remasters on a USB drive (a compilation of high-quality digital remasters which retails for around £200).

Within this tightly controlled reworking and reframing of the Beatles' work, the company has been careful to impose and maintain a clear and coherent narrative of the band's career. Their roots within the city are a clear constant within the endlessly retold 'official' story of the band, in which the 'working class', 'gritty' and 'industrial' aspects of the city are at the fore. For example, the visual imagery used across the event releases for the 1995 *Beatles Anthology* was accompanied by the single 'Free as a Bird', a recording produced from a 1977 John Lennon demo which was trailed as the first 'new' recording by the band since their split in 1970. The video for 'Free as a Bird' has the Beatles as dockers in the thriving port of Liverpool, and includes street scenes clearly meant to represent another era. The centrality and longevity of this type of representation is illustrated by the high-profile September 2009 launch of the cross-platform console game *Beatles Rock Band*. The opening cinematic for the game uses a similar set of images: panning down from Liverpool's iconic skyline through rows of closely packed smoky terraces into back-streets (perhaps in a deliberate reference to *Yellow Submarine*), eventually descending into the Cavern Club, before opening out into a montage of the band's iconic career moments (Shea Stadium, the *Abbey Road* cover and a surreal landscape inspired by the band's psychedelic period). Despite their apparent affection, these nostalgic and stylized versions of the city also paint a picture of urban decline and the economic and cultural forces that were to factor in the depopulation of the city. The mythical Liverpool consistently linked to the group was far from a centre of cultural dynamism and creativity, but was rather a place which these most sophisticated and urbane of popular musicians clearly transcended and quickly outgrew.

Post-punk and urban decline

Subsequent generations of Liverpool musicians have been equally reflective of the city within their work. However, unlike the Beatles, many of the city's post-punk and indie artists of the 1980s sought to reflect the material conditions of the city from within. These groups also had a new set of nationally mediated cultural associations to contend with. Liverpool was 'othered' within the UK media on the basis of its notorious social, economic and political problems. During the 1980s the city became known as much for urban decline as for football and the Beatles. The British media used the city as a symbol not just of urban decay but of everything that had gone wrong with the nation's cities (Cohen 2007: 42) and represented the city through stereotypes of white, working-class belligerency, thus enhancing the marginality of a city that had once played such a central role in the global economy and global popular culture.

It is unsurprising therefore that numerous artists of the period engaged with debates about the city's image, identity and its social, economic and political problems, albeit in a number of differing ways. From chart hits such as the Christians' 'Forgotten Town' and Wah!'s 'Story of the Blues' and 'Come Back', through to the gallows humour of Birkenhead cult band Half Man Half Biscuit and lesser-known tracks such as Cook Da Books' Toxteth-riot-inspired 'Piggy in the Middle', the city's musical output during this period was often acutely concerned with the wider effects of the city's decline (Strachan and Cohen 2005; Cohen 2007). Shack's 1988 debut album *Zilch*, for instance, includes tracks such as 'High Rise Low Life', a rather beautiful pop song about the isolation of estate living, and 'Who Killed Clayton Square', which uses the city planners' destruction of Liverpool's Victorian core as a metaphor for the city's wider decline. The band would continue this strain of realism to great effect in their later work, particularly the folky-sounding 'Streets of Kenny', which refers to the particularly run-down Liverpool area of Kensington and its heroin problems.

However, Liverpool's experiences of decline and vulnerability and its negative mediation within the UK have served to reinforce common expressions of local resilience and pride that are central to its collective memory. Despite the stark, often negative representations of Liverpool in the city's post-punk music, earlier strains of representation continued to persist. For instance, the themes of innovation, creativity and the spirit of Liverpool people have been mined (in their later work at least) by post-punk songwriters Pete Wylie and Ian McNabb, whose 'Heart as Big as Liverpool' and 'Liverpool Girl' both tap into the vein of sentimental representation that pervaded many of the city's musical cultures described above. Even in McNabb's lament for the decline of the city, the Icicle Works' 'Up Here in the North of England', with its imagery of children putting 'smack in your veins', there is an ironic nod to the city's national image, a cultural heritage of televised comedians and 'off-beat love affairs'.

Sonic heritage

It should be noted that such lyrical representations are not the only way in which collective memory is constructed through the city's popular music. There are also very specific musical continuities which provide a sonic heritage that serves to construct and maintain identities. Although Cohen (2007) carefully problematizes the notion of an essence of a Liverpool sound, there are nonetheless distinct strains within the city's musical output which are significant. For example, Cohen (2007: 45) herself points to a 'notable taste for psychedelia and a prevalence of bands producing a lush, guitar based and pop influenced style of rock characterised by a strong emphasis on melody' during the 1980s. We can understand this predilection as being grounded within a set of prevalent social practices which ultimately lead to a particular set of sounds being associated with the city's music. In broad terms, melodic 1980s pop such as that produced by the Lotus Eaters, Black and China Crisis, who had success on a national level, along with bands such as the Pale Fountains, Afraid of Mice, 16 Tambourines, and Up and Running, who had a high degree of local popularity, drew upon and perpetuated Liverpool's successful pop heritage. In addition, the city's musical continuities have been supported and passed on through distinct listening and performance practices rooted in a cultural context specific to Liverpool.

For example, musically, bands such as Shack, the Stairs and the La's took a perceived golden age of 1960s rock, pop and psychedelia as a musical template for their work. The musical and stylistic make-up of these groups was itself rooted in an idiosyncratic youth movement within the city that can be distinguished from subcultural practice in the rest of the country. As Peter Hooton, lead singer of the Farm, notes (in Hewitson 2008: 129–36), in the early 1980s what became known as 'retro-scally' culture began to emerge. Evolving from (and as a reaction to the popularization of) a distinct terrace culture, the retro-scally scene in the city mixed the football casuals' obsession with clothes and football[9] with drug use and an appreciation of various types of retro music forms. Scene participants wore variations on classic British looks, with tweed, corduroy, Barbour jackets and Hush Puppies (among many other style choices), moving in and out of fashion at an often dizzying pace. As Hooton documents (in Hewitson 2008: 130), these young people 'also looked back to the previous generation's music collections', to artists such as Pink Floyd, Simon and Garfunkel, Frank Zappa and Roy Harper; 'any group that you could "buzz" off was sought after and proclaimed as "better"'. Initially, pub bands such as Groundpig, Deja Vu and Drama garnered big followings among this crowd, playing cover versions of well known folk rock, psychedelic, classic rock and progressive rock tracks (Hewitson 2008: 130; see also Du Noyer 2002: 184), but the stylistic and musical preoccupations of retro-scally eventually began to feed into the city's original bands. Records such as the Stairs' paean to marijuana 'Weedbus' and the La's debut album, with its coded allusions to heroin in their best-known track 'There She Goes' and the dole queue depression song 'Doledrums', specifically sought to plot the lifestyle of unemployed young men in the city while being musically rooted in the preference for retro sounds that had become prominent within this strand of the city's youth culture.

Hooton's own band, the Farm, was among the first to connect this youth culture with music, both in its visual image and through *The End*, a fanzine covering casual culture to which they regularly contributed. The band gained a strong following both in Liverpool and with other football casual scenes across the north, such as that in Leeds (see Long and Williams 2006: 17). At a similar time the La's (whose name celebrated the scouse pronunciation of 'lads') mixed the retro-scally look with a 'retro' style recalling the 1960s and reflecting the conscious influence on their music of beat music, skiffle, psychedelia and garage rock. This hybrid musical and visual style became a template for later Liverpool acts, from 1980s and 1990s groups such as Smaller, Top, Shack, Rain, the Hoovers, and the Real People, through to acts of the 2000s such as the Coral and the Zutons. We can, in effect, trace a continuity of musical practices in dialogue with each other (that is, they are informed by and build upon past musical works), which accounts for a continuation and construction of musical meaning relating to the city and its history. This musical and stylistic continuity over two decades further served to cement the idea within wider media accounts (especially in the music and style press) of Liverpool as a source of a distinct and organic working-class popular culture.

Around 2001, the Coral (a band signed with Deltasonic/Sony), from Hoylake on the Wirral, began to receive considerable promotion in the national press and heavy radio coverage in the UK. The band was marketed as spearheading a resurgence in the city's musical culture, based around a particular club night called the Bandwagon, which regularly hosted gigs by a number of like-minded local bands, such as the Zutons, Tramp Attack, the Bandits, the Hokum Clones and the Stands. Most of these acts drew upon a similar lineage of prescribed musical reference points which have become associated with the city and its musicians over a number of years (late-1960s West Coast rock, psychedelia, blues, country and skiffle, along with prominent Liverpool acts of the last twenty years which had used similar music, most notably the La's, Shack and the Stairs). Added to this, the work of these bands often engaged thematically with Liverpool's heritage as a seaport and its historical connections with North America. The Coral's 'Spanish Main', the Bandits' 'Once Upon a Time' and the Zutons' 'Railroad' evoke a surreal folk memory of seafaring and a mythology of working-class migrant labour, while the musical grounding within country music of tracks such as the Zutons' 'Moons and Horror Shows' and the Stands' 'I Need You' recall an older strain in Liverpool's musical heritage – the city's reputation as the 'Nashville of the north' (McManus 1994; Cohen 2007; Brocken 2010).

The way in which these acts were represented in the media also drew upon this cultural heritage. Coverage of Liverpool bands in the early 2000s was underpinned by a connection to place with a very specific set of reference points relating to Liverpool, its musical heritage and particular perceptions of its culture. Journalists often used 'scouse' (see for example *NME* 2003), or derivations of the word, as the primary adjective to describe this new wave of bands: 'cosmic scouse' (Moody 2003: 51), 'psychedelic Scouse urchins' (Price 2003), 'scary scouse shroomadelacists' (*NME* 2004) and 'cosmic scallies' (Du Noyer 2007: 250). Petridis, writing in the *Guardian*, even explicitly positioned the bands as 'products of Liverpool's cultural isolation' (Petridis 2002). Many reviews and interviews with Liverpool bands of the time also made direct reference to their alleged use of marijuana, ecstasy or LSD 'scouse smarties' (Ahmed 2002; Beaumont 2003, 2004). While the use of these recreational drugs is not uncommon among musicians, the inclusion of drug references within coverage of Liverpool bands was marked by its regularity and inevitability. Ahmed's (2004) reference to 'A gaggle of scousers ... in the stoned circle' at Glastonbury was typical. Journalists also constantly framed these acts with reference to a local musical heritage, naming artists such as John Lennon, Shack, the La's, the Beatles, Echo and the Bunnymen and Wah!, or describing their music in terms of 'sea shanties' (Kessler 2002; Ahmed 2003; Nicholson 2004). A typical example of the way these bands were received is given in a retrospective of the band the Coral in the local listings magazine *Inform*:

> It wasn't that they were the most extraordinary band Liverpool has produced for years, it was that they were every band Liverpool has produced. The eponymous album was like a Liverpudlian greatest hits wherein you got bits of the Beatles, the Teardrops, Echo and the Bunnymen, the Stairs, Dr Phibes, Shack, the Living Brain ... even Mr Ray's Wig World. They also have a healthy dose of bands much loved by Scousers, such as Pink Floyd and Captain Beefheart. Most of all they were riding the current love of 'shanty music' in Liverpool. (*Inform* 2003)

These Liverpool acts of the 2000s provide an interesting articulation of the connections between music and place. In effect, both musically and in terms of their image and mediation, they are reliant upon a whole host of musical and cultural associations that have accumulated over a number of decades. They both draw upon and are in dialogue with a cultural heritage, which, although open to challenge, is nonetheless undeniably powerful. The particular configuration of psychedelia, skiffle, drug culture and working-class youth cultures utilized by these bands was coupled with a folk memory of the city's maritime past and cosmopolitanism to create a movement which was understood as distinctly Liverpudlian.

Conclusion

This chapter has traced the representation of Liverpool and its cultural associations through the songs, recordings and cultures of its popular musicians. The legacy afforded by the representation of Liverpool within its popular music provides a powerful set of associations which have served to construct and reinforce collective memory. While representations of the city in song should always be contextualized within wider trends, relating to genre and national and international movements in popular music culture, the strands within Liverpool music described here do constitute something specific and locally grounded. Indeed, while bands such as the Beatles have carried with them national and international representations of Liverpool, there is a concurrent set of locally specific narratives which are important within popular culture within the city itself. In many cases, local acclaim is reinforced over time, maintaining distinct and self-reflexive notions of musical identity within the city. For example, bands which weren't necessarily critically or commercially acclaimed on a national level have maintained a key importance within Liverpool's musical cultures and individual songs have maintained local popularity over a number of years. Locally popular songs, such as Up and Running's 'Johnny and Marie', are regularly played on local radio stations BBC Radio Merseyside and Radio City, and acts such as Deaf School, Edgar Jones, Mick Head and Thomas Lang are afforded an importance within the city's music scenes way above their impact on the international musical landscape. Hence, in the same way as Belcham (2000) notes an exceptionalism in Liverpool culture more generally, we can identify a musical exceptionalism whereby these locally significant moments are remembered, recalled and maintained within the conversation that the city has about itself.

Hence, there is a duality to the way in which the city's popular music contributes to collective memory both at a national and at an international level and within the city's distinct discourses of the local. These representations overlap and are in constant dialogue with each other. Lipsitz (1990) sees popular music as a dialogic form, in that recorded music is involved in a continual dialogue with other musical works and past musicians. As well as responding to answer, correct, silence or extend a previous work, new songs and recordings inform future work and are continually informed by previous work. He argues that 'while no cultural form has a fixed political meaning, rock and roll music has been and continues to be a dialogic space, an arena where memories of the past serve to critique and change the present' (Lipsitz 1990: 132). While the examples given in this chapter serve to illustrate how the city's musicians address the material conditions of Liverpool and draw upon its history, they also have a cumulative effect, contributing to a discursive space within a wider collective memory. The narratives about the city described within this chapter build up in a process of historical accretion which has an active effect upon the way in which the city and its culture are understood through the constant reinforcement of a musical legacy. Ultimately, utterances about the city in song and through the mediation of its musicians have to be understood within a wider framework, in that they are always in dialogue with existing representations to form part of a cumulative discourse about the city. This dialogic function of popular music within collective memory is highly pertinent within the context of Liverpool. Its self-image as a musical city has cemented the idea of music as a space where identities are forged and negotiated. As Belcham (2000: 60) notes, 'music offers perhaps the best insight into Liverpool's distinctiveness or "otherness"'.

Notes

1   *Yellow Submarine* (1968). Animated feature film. Directed by George Dunning. King Features Entertainment, Subafilms, Apple Films, TV Cartoons.
2   *Five Television Screenplays* (1982). Directed by Philip Saville, BBC Pebble Mill.
3   Film (1985). Directed by Peter Smith. No Surrender Films, Dumbarton Films, National Film Finance Corporation, Film Four International, Lauron International.
4   Although it should be noted that *In My Life* was considered controversial at the time because of its use of pop material and pop-style strings on some of the arrangements.
5   The light-hearted musical settings of Scaffold and Beatles recordings also tap into the perception that people from Liverpool have a natural and ready comic wit which marks them out from the general populace.
6   I am referring to the 1960s and 1970s here, as there had been an earlier tradition of regional accents in British popular music, as evidenced by performers such as George Formby and Gracie Fields, whose Lancashire accents were clearly part of their enormous public appeal in the 1930s and 1940s.
7   *The Beatles Story*. Capitol. 1964.
8   *Beat City* (1963). Television programme. Directed by Charlie Squires. Rediffusion.
9   The street style that became known as 'casual' evolved among football fans in the late 1970s, led most prominently by followers of the big city teams of the north-west of England. Both Liverpool and Everton fans were instrumental in the development of this style, introducing fashions, labels and sportswear brought home from away trips following their teams in European competitions. From these trips a competitive street culture developed based around the ownership of exclusive brands or individual items of clothing that were difficult to obtain in the UK (see Hewitson 2008).

References

Ahmed, Imran (2002) 'The Zutons: Merseyside Keeps 'Em Coming'. *NME*, 14 September. p. 27.
Ahmed, Imran (2003) 'The League of Extraordinary Gentlemen'. *NME*, 26 July. pp. 27–28.
Ahmed, Imran (2004) 'Mersey Feat'. *NME*, 28 June. p. 39.

Asserman, Jan (1995) 'Collective Memory and Cultural Identity'. *New German Critique* 65: 125–33.

Beaumont, Mark (2003) 'Wagons Roll-Up'. *NME*, 5 July. p. 21.

Beaumont, Mark (2004) Review of the Zutons' 'Confusion'. *NME*, 11 December. p. 61.

Belcham, John (2000) *Merseypride: Essays in Liverpool Exceptionalism*. Liverpool: Liverpool University Press.

Bolland, Philip (2010) 'Sonic Geography, Place and Race in the Formation of Local Identity: Liverpool and Scousers'. *Geografiska Annaler: Series B, Human Geography* 92(1): 1–22.

Brocken, Michael (2003) *The British Folk Revival 1944–2002*. Aldershot: Ashgate.

Brocken, Michael (2010) *Other Voices: Hidden Histories of Liverpool's Popular Music Scenes, 1930s–1970s*. Aldershot: Ashgate.

Cohen, Sara (2003) 'Community'. In: John Shepherd, David Horn and Dave Laing (eds) *The Continuum Encyclopedia of Popular Music of the World. Volume I: Media, Industry and Society*. London: Continuum. pp. 183–86.

Cohen, Sara (2007) *Decline, Renewal and the City in Popular Music Culture: Beyond the Beatles*. Aldershot: Ashgate.

Confino, Alon (1997) 'Collective Memory and Cultural History'. *American Historical Review* 102(5): 1386–403.

Daniels, Stephen (2006) 'Suburban Pastoral: Strawberry Fields Forever and Sixties Memory'. *Cultural Geographies* 13(1): 28–54.

Doerflinger, William Main (1951) *Songs of the Sailor and Lumberman*. New York: Macmillan.

Du Noyer, Paul (2002) *Liverpool: Wondrous Place – Music from the Cavern to Cream*. London: Virgin.

Du Noyer, Paul (2007) 'Subversive Dreamers: Liverpool Songwriting from the Beatles to the Zutons'. In: Michael Murphy and Deryn Rees-Jones (eds) *Writing Liverpool: Essays and Interviews*. Liverpool: Liverpool University Press. pp. 239–51.

Green, Nick (2005) 'Songs from the Wood and Sounds of the Suburbs: A Folk, Rock and Punk Portrait of England, 1965–1977'. *Built Environment* 31(3): 255–70.

Hewitson, Dave (2008) *The Liverpool Boys Are Back in Town: The Birth of Terrace Culture*. Liverpool: Bluecoat Press.

Honeybone, Patrick (2007) 'New Dialect Formation in Nineteenth-Century Liverpool: A Brief History of Scouse'. In: Anthony Grant and Clive Grey (eds) *The Mersey Sound: Liverpool's Language, People and Place*. West Kirby: Open House Press. pp. 106–40.

Inform (2003) 'The Coral'. *Inform*, December 2003. p. 8.

Kessler, Ted (2002) 'The Rebirth of "Pool"'. *NME*, 12 January. p. 15.

Lipsitz, George (1990) *Time Passages: Collective Memory and American Popular Culture*. Minneapolis, MN: University of Minnesota Press.

Long, Cathy and John Williams (2006) 'Football and Music Cultures in Liverpool'. *Esporte e Sociedade* 1: 1–43.

McManus, Kevin (1994) *Nashville of the North: Country Music in Liverpool*. Liverpool: Institute of Popular Music, University of Liverpool.

Middleton, Richard (1990) *Studying Popular Music*. Milton Keynes: Open University Press.

Moody, Paul (2003) 'The Review: Singles'. *NME*, 22 November. pp. 50–51.

Nicholson, Barry (2004) 'No Shrooms 'Til Brooklyn!' *NME*, 23 October. p. 27.

NME (2003) 'The *NME* Artist Directory'. *NME*, 27 September. p. 12.

NME (2004) 'Burn It: The Zutons'. *NME*, 8 May. p. 10.

O'Neill, Francis (1907) *The Dance Music of Ireland: 10,001 Gems of Irish Melody.* New York: Regan

Petridis, Alex (2002) 'The Fab Six'. *Guardian,* 19 July. p. 19 (review section).

Pickering, Michael and Emily Keightley (2006) 'The Modalities of Nostalgia'. *Current Sociology* 54(6): 919–41.

Price, Simon (2003) 'The Coral: Electric Ballroom London'. *Independent on Sunday*, 27 July.

Sheff, David (1981) 'The Playboy Interview: John Lennon'. *Playboy* 28(1): 75–114.

Sommers Smith, Sally K. (1998) 'Landscape and Memory in Irish Traditional Music'. *New Hibernia Review / Iris Éireannach Nua* 2(1): 132–44.

Strachan, Robert (2009) '"Where Do I Begin the Story?" Collective Memory, Biographical Authority and the Rock Biography'. *Popular Music History* 3(1): 65–80

Strachan, Rob and Sara Cohen (2005) 'Music Cultures and the Appropriation of Urban Space'. In: Philip Oswalt (ed.) *Shrinking Cities, Vol. 1: International Investigation*. Ostfildern: Hatje Cantz Verlag. pp. 398–431.

Tatom Letts, Marianne (2008) 'Sky of Blue, Sea of Green: A Semiotic Reading of the Film *Yellow Submarine*'. *Popular Music* 27(1): 1–14.

Van Dijck, Jose (2006) 'Record and Hold: Popular Music Between Personal and Collective Memory'. *Critical Studies in Media Communication* 23(5): 357–74.

CHAPTER 4

Pubs in the precinct: music making, retail developments and the characterization of urban space

Sara Cohen and Brett Lashua

Introduction: Liverpool from the 'Big Dig' to the 'Big Gig'

In January 2008, as Liverpool kicked off its year as European Capital of Culture (ECoC) with a 'People's Opening' event, we stood amidst a vast crowd that filled the streets in front of the city's grand, historic St George's Hall. Ringo Starr was performing, among others, on the roof of the hall that night and a huge audience had gathered, stretching several blocks back, past the arches of Lime Street station, Liverpool's primary rail terminus. In fact, we were so far from the main performance area at St George's that we preferred to view events as they were projected onto the facade of St Johns precinct, a monolithic modernist retail block situated directly opposite Lime Street station. On this night, as throughout the year, Liverpool celebrated its 'renaissance', marking a transformation through physical regeneration – that is, the 'Big Dig', a massive reconstruction of the city centre[I] – as well as its cultural renaissance – that is, the 'Big Gig', its year in the spotlight as ECoC.

During the 'People's Opening' on that chilly January night, the city showcased its musical and civic heritage, from Ringo and the Beatles to newer rock and pop groups such as the Wombats (who also performed atop St George's Hall). As we stood and watched events unfold, the brutalist concrete facade of St Johns precinct provided little more than a backdrop for the main show. Moreover, during subsequent months the precinct seemed to slip increasingly into the background of the city centre as the newly built 'Liverpool One' shopping development took shape, extending the boundaries of city's main shopping district and shifting its focal point further away from the precinct and towards the River Mersey. Indeed, as the ECoC year progressed, much of St Johns precinct was concealed behind a ring of steel trusses, wrapped in an 'artistic' purple membrane, and eclipsed by the installation of what was reported in the media to be Europe's largest television screen.

Although overshadowed by the historic St George's Hall and the brand new Liverpool One retail development, St Johns precinct has its own stories to tell, its own unique musical character and histories. During the 1970s it had a rooftop ballroom, while down underground its basement was the site of three pub rock venues. These three venues are the foci of this chapter. The chapter uses the precinct and its pubs as a case study through which to explore music's role and significance in the characterization of urban space, and to highlight interconnections between shifting landscapes of music performance and retail development. The discussion draws upon interviews with some of the musicians who used to perform in the precinct, as well as upon archival and historical materials, including newspaper accounts, maps and photographs.

We begin by describing the precinct pub venues and drawing on this description to consider the role of musicians, music and music making in the characterization of urban space. We then situate the precinct and its pubs within a wider context of urban regeneration, examining the planning and development of the precinct in order to reflect on the relationship between music making and the increasing emphasis on retail-led regeneration in British cities. This will help to show that while musicians and music making may influence and characterize urban space, they are at the same time influenced by urban change and by regeneration initiatives that transform the physical urban environment. We end the chapter by relating our discussion of the precinct and its pubs to notions of 'heritage', history and local distinctiveness. In particular, we situate memories of the musical past in relation to official constructions of Liverpool's music heritage, and consider St Johns precinct as just one of many

Liverpool venues and locations that were centres for different kinds of music but have remained relatively marginal and overlooked with regard to official accounts of Liverpool music history. In doing so we show how such 'hidden' histories can provide valuable insights into not only the music in Liverpool during particular historical eras, but also the conditions at those times (Moore 2006).

St Johns precinct and the 1970s pub rock scene

When St Johns precinct was officially opened by the Queen in April 1971 its basement housed three pub venues – the Moonstone, the Sportsman, and the Star and Garter. There was also the Top Rank Suite ballroom above the precinct's car park. Throughout the 1970s the pubs provided popular venues for Liverpool's rock music scene, staging performances by local and visiting bands and providing spaces in which musicians could hang out and interact. The most enduring memories of all three pub venues were of the perceived calibre of musicians who performed there, which made the precinct an outstanding place at that time, as well as of how these pubs were places for certain groups of fans. Most of the musicians we spoke to associated the precinct and its venues with a high standard of musicianship and described it as certainly a place for musicians to see, and be seen by, other musicians. We now provide a sense of how some of these musicians described, remembered and engaged with these pubs, associating each with its own distinctive character.

The Moonstone

During the early 1970s the Moonstone was associated with progressive and folk rock bands, and featured performances by groups such as Wildlife, Skyfall, Superstride, Ulysses, Colonel Bagshot and Thunderboots. One musician explained:

> MIKE, GUITARIST: The Moonstone was different altogether. It was more like a hippy hangout. If you were going to stop off at the precinct before going somewhere else, you'd stop off at the Moonstone for a drink, not the Sportsman. I spent around four years going there as a punter. It was like a trog [a local name for hippy] emporium. They'd burn incense and people would be wearing a lot of musk – that trog oil[2] smell.

Another musician told us:

PAUL, KEYBOARDIST: It was quite dark in there – they kept it dark for some reason, so it had a bit of a dark atmosphere [laughs], not like the Star and Garter, which was a bit more bright and welcoming, and the Sportsman was a bit more classy, or at least purveyed itself as classy – the Moonstone was pretty underground – I mean, it *was* underground, but it had the sort of feel … it had the underground atmosphere. Initially I thought it was quite disconcerting, unfriendly – until I got sort of used to it, and then, of course, it was gradually changing anyway – it started becoming a lot more popular … the one I always particularly remember is the Moonstone…. I think we played there a lot more than any other band – we were called Ulysses by that time – we used to play something like twice a week. Partly because the guy that ran it would ring us up and say 'Someone hasn't turned up'!

By the mid-1970s the Moonstone is remembered as being more of a heavy rock venue, epitomized by bands such as the Liverpool-based Nutz and their second incarnation as Rage.

More than one musician commented that the venue had a certain atmosphere:

PAUL, KEYBOARDIST: There was an alternative vibe there; because the Moonstone was fairly new it had an alternative vibe, a different vibe.

There was no immediate access from the street into the Moonstone. To reach the pub, musicians had to enter the precinct and move a little distance along a corridor. Once inside, the Moonstone was spread out on two floors:

PHIL, DRUMMER: The first floor was like a bar but there was another floor underneath. You'd go down the stairs, which were quite windy. The bar was to the right. It was another longish bar that was curved at the end. The bar would go off and curve at the end and a lot of people would congregate at the end.

PAUL, KEYBOARDIST: [It] was an odd-shaped room but it worked quite well. It was a long corridor-shaped room. You came downstairs and there were booths on the left and the bar on the right. At the end there was a stage on the right, which was right next to the bar.

TONY, DRUMMER: There was a jukebox – a really powerful jukebox, really really good.

MIKE, GUITARIST: The band played at the far end on a small stage, and to the left was a seated area – '70s, curbed, plush seating made of nylon that got all sticky on your legs – horrible. You'd see similar characters there.

There seems to be some debate on the colour scheme of the pub, but the general consensus is that the walls were dark and painted either purple or deep maroon.

Beyond the physical fabric of the venue, it had a musical import-ance. One guitarist said: 'I'd go religiously to the Moonstone to see guitarists and I learned a lot from them and it helped me to develop as a musician.' Another important aspect of the social fabric of the Moonstone appears to have been a sense of belonging to a music 'scene' or 'community', as illustrated by the following comments:

MOONSTONE PATRON: I followed all the bands in the '70s with my boyfriend and we went to a lot of these pubs. My favourite bands back then were Thunderboots, Export, Rocking Horse, Liverpool Express and Nutz. I suppose I was a bit of a hairy, a rocker as they called us back then. I remember talking to the drummer from Nutz (I fancied him) and also the drummer from Export (I also fancied him). They were so nice and people seemed much more friendlier then, especially in the music circle. I had many a good time at the Moonstone, [and] although a selective audience, it was something special.[3]

MIKE, GUITARIST: The Moonstone was a watering hole for people who would otherwise be persecuted. Liverpool could be a hateful fucking place for anyone who was a bit different.

All the people we spoke with remember the Moonstone as being well attended and it was clearly very popular. One musician who had a mid-week residency there in 1973/74 remembered that 'the place would fill up and become crammed' and 'You couldn't get to the bar it was so packed'. Yet today there is no trace of the Moonstone in St Johns precinct. Parts of the space it once occupied were converted into a shoe shop, which had ceased trading by the end of 2008, while other parts were turned into storage.

The Sportsman

Remembering his early days as a drummer in Liverpool during the 1960s and 1970s, one musician connected the Sportsman to a particular moment in time when he sensed that Liverpool's musical landscape had noticeably changed:

PHIL, DRUMMER: I can't think of any pubs that had bands on. I think it was only the early seventies that that started to change, when pubs all of a sudden were putting bands on, you know, and there were actual pub gigs … I first sort of remember the Sportsman as being the first main one, as far as I know, in town … it had a stage and curtains, [and] although they didn't use the curtains, it was like made for watching a band. The whole thing was set up just right.

When I say they didn't have bands on, not in the way we think of bands, you know, setting up, bringing a PA. They would have had entertainment which could have been a band but there was nowhere for them. They literally would have been told to squash in that corner because you're not the priority.... They'd have sat in a corner, and played all night … and someone could have said, sing, you know, sing Peggy Sue, and they would have done it, and then they would have had a drink and then they would have just played but you didn't think of it as being a pub band: it was a pub that had entertainment and that entertainment could be a sing-along, it could be five people with guitars, or one. And I mean I actually do remember doing a gig in a pub with just a snare drum and sitting there – and there was a door there and a door there and I sat in this wedge with just a snare drum. For a PA we used a tape recorder with a tape recorder mike so the speaker would have been what – two watts? And a guitar and that was it. And, you know, no one took any notice of us, so you couldn't say that that was a pub band; it was just a pub that gave a pound or something to these guys and, you know, and that was it. So I always think of the Sportsman really as being the first one that actually physically put a group on with a PA and presented it.

Like the Moonstone, the Sportsman was also underground, down a set of winding steps. However, there was direct access to it from Roe Street, very near to the city's main bus terminus, at Queen Square. This distinguished it from the Moonstone, which required a long walk into the precinct, which some musicians found a bit scary, as they were afraid of being mugged late at night in a deserted corridor. However, both venues benefited from their proximity to central transportation links and were easily accessible:

PHIL, DRUMMER: The Sportsman was on the outside of the precinct. You didn't have to go in the precinct to go to it. You could just pull up outside then and just walk in the door, whereas I think there was a pub inside [the Moonstone] … in like the bowels of the precinct. But I think the great thing with the Sportsman was, it was on the outside and although you had to go downstairs, it still felt accessible and easy to come and go to. There was a whole row of bus-stops outside on both sides because the old bus station was right outside.

As the name implies, the Sportsman was done out in sports and horse-racing décor, described by one musician:

MIKE, GUITARIST: All very brown – turf colours, and the décor was kitted out like a bar at Aintree racecourse. And that might have been the thinking behind it. Ravenseft [the developers] might have had the idea of a sports/horse-type bar right by Lime Street station and all the bus routes. It was quite sophisticated – it had a carpet – but by the mid-1970s you'd be sticking to the carpet.

Mike went on to describe the layout as follows:

There was one large bar. You came in and on the left hand side there was a large bar in front of you. The band played to the right of the bar. The fashion in the '70s was for long bars.... Each of those pub bars in the precinct had them. It was considered to be a bit sophisticated – too many US films being watched.

Other musicians recall that there was a racing car hung upside down as they entered the pub, and people often tried to climb up and sit in it, upside down, which led to various funny mishaps.

One of the musicians who regularly played at the venue remembered that the thing that stood out the most for him was that the Sportsman had seating both in front of and behind the stage. He recalled that the serious musicians could congregate in the area behind the stage as the band played, and see very closely what the band was doing. According to one drummer, Tony, 'The Sportsman was the place to go on Sunday night. I never missed Supercharge.'

And, indeed, mention of the Sportsman rarely seemed to come up without the name of Supercharge. Supercharge was a boogie-woogie rhythm and blues band that had a residency at the Sportsman on Sunday and Monday nights from 1973 to 1975. The band signed to Virgin Records in the mid-1970s and did much touring around the UK university circuit. The group notably opened for Queen in 1976 at an outdoor gig in Hyde Park, where singer/saxophonist Albie Donnelly reportedly went on stage wearing the same style of skin-tight lycra suit that Freddie Mercury wore on the same stage later in the day. The band members were known as jokers but were also admired for their musicianship:

MIKE, GUITARIST: Supercharge were really a super group – the best of Liverpool's R'n'B musicians come together.... They were R'n'B, funk and soul…. They knew their dots [that is, they could read music] – they were skilled, highly trained musicians.

I kind of admired them as a muso group. But I never crossed the door of the Sportsman other than for that. Liverpool didn't really like us. I found it far easier to get around Birkenhead,[4] which was more rock-oriented and had places to go and pubs with live music on. Whereas in Liverpool live music was being strangulated by disco. It was pre-disco but the DJ was ousting groups left, right and centre. So it was quite unusual to have a group like Supercharge in the city centre.

Another musician told us:

The Sportsman was slightly more upmarket. You went there and sat down. It was also slightly more mainstream – Supercharge played there…. You wouldn't mind taking a girlfriend there, whereas the Moonstone was more grungy.

Again, despite the strong memories of the people who attended, there is little trace of the pub within St Johns precinct today and the space that the Sportsman had occupied has since been converted into storage.

The Star and Garter

The Star and Garter seems to have been the least memorable of the three precinct pub venues for most of the musicians we spoke with, but even so, it was often described as being a great room with a packed house. One musician recalled that it was brighter and more welcoming than the other precinct venues. Another remembered it as having an L-shaped room and said that when certain bands were on you just couldn't move. Like the other precinct venues, the stage area was relatively small; hence one photograph of the group School for Girls performing at the Star and Garter in 1979 shows the band's equipment filling the stage and spilling into adjacent areas.

One guitarist remembered the Star and Garter as being 'horrible. Flock wallpaper – a cod plastic and fake wood version of a London pub. It was kind of lightweight music.' However, the Sportsman was usually described to us as being 'more rock' in style than the other two precinct pubs. One drummer remembered that 'The Star and Garter was more for cover bands[5] and rock/pop bands', and mentioned the band called Export, which used to play regularly at the Star and Garter and went on to sign with Epic Records and to become 'big in the US'. Another musician told us: 'I played there with another band later in the '70s, late '70s. That was more of a rocky type venue I think.'

Again, the access and entrance to the pub were remembered as being significant:

PAUL, KEYBOARDIST: The Star and Garter was round on Lime Street wasn't it ... where the entrance is to the St George Hotel now; it was round there, but you could just walk straight in and again down the stairs, but they, I think, were again fortunate that they were on the outside of the precinct so you didn't have to walk into alleyways or anything to get to it. It was there, the sign was there, although it was down.... They didn't have as big a stage and it wasn't as big.... I know for some bands who were really popular there, it was great, you know. There was one band, School for Girls, if you went down, they really like pulled in a great crowd and it was always packed but I never ever liked it as much as the Sportsman. Just didn't have the atmosphere ... the Sportsman got far more in and had the better atmosphere. Too claustrophobic, I think, the Star and Garter. And also I think it was a bit rougher in a way.

Like the Sportsman, there was access from the street down into the Star and Garter, which was also situated directly opposite Lime Street station. Along with the other pub venues it remained in operation through most of the 1980s before conversion into shops and storage spaces.

Music, music making and the characterization of urban space

We have so far pointed to ways in which the precinct pubs have been described to us by some of the musicians who performed in them. These descriptions help to illustrate how musicians and music making produce and characterize urban space. Social, spatial and aesthetic factors have combined in the memories of the musicians we interviewed to give each of the pubs a distinctive character and feel. Yet the three venues were nevertheless closely connected to each other, and together they helped to characterize the precinct basement as a distinctive musical space and to make it both a landmark for many local musicians and also, given its association with contemporary popular music sounds, a 'soundmark'.

During the early to mid-1970s it was common for the same musicians to perform in all three pubs, and for musicians to drift in and out of them in order to catch the different bands on stage during any one night. According to one musician, 'At all three venues, musicians went there to see other musicians.' Another musician told us, 'It was great because you could just walk across and see your mates in the other pubs and listen to the bands. It was like a triangle of venues.' The musicians also performed in each other's bands and met at the precinct to exchange music-related information and gossip. One drummer told us, 'There were more than those three venues but they were the places that everyone would go to. I never took a girlfriend there because I'd be talking so much business in those three pubs.' He and the other musicians we have spoken to continued to gain employment as musicians after they stopped frequenting the precinct, and also went on to run their own music businesses and music training courses.

The precinct thus provided a fertile training ground in live music performance and opportunities for the development of contacts and careers in music. The three pubs gained a reputation as spaces for musicians and musicianship. One guitarist we spoke to associated the Moonstone with a high standard of musicianship, describing it as 'the hardest gig to get in Liverpool' and therefore something to aim for, adding that the music performed there 'broke new ground'. In 1984 the Moonstone pub was renamed Mylo's, out of respect for one local musician, the drummer John Mylett. Mylett had performed regularly at the venue with the local heavy rock bands Nutz and Rage but was killed in a traffic accident. As a venue, Mylo's thus provided a physical idiom for defining a particular group of music makers and the relationships between them, and for expressing feelings of belonging to that group and to a wider music 'scene' or 'community'.

Nutz and other bands that performed at the precinct during this period did not achieve lasting national or international notoriety but many released albums. They also performed regularly in Britain, Europe and further afield, and supported internationally known artists. The precinct was thus just one site within the wider performance 'circuit' of these musicians. It was also just one stop along their regular routes to and around Liverpool city centre. In fact, our interviewees made a point of telling us how accessible the precinct was, given its location right by the city's main railway station and central bus terminal, and the fact that it had its own multi-storey car park:

MIKE, GUITARIST: When I moved to Birkenhead in 1971 I was amazed at how many people from there went like I did to the Cavern and Moonstone. We all got off at the same place in Liverpool and all got the same tunnel bus back home.

Moreover, as the precinct was located within a central entertainment district, musicians could easily move on from it to nearby pubs and clubs.

The precinct was thus a social hub, dwelling and stopping-off point for musicians who helped to characterize it as a youthful, musical space. By travelling to and occupying the pub venues these musicians contributed not just to the social life of the precinct but also to the social dynamics, rhythms and transient micro-topographies of the area in which it was situated, helping to characterize it as a central entertainment space. Music making, as Ruth Finnegan (1989), points out, constitutes an extensive but in many ways 'hidden' field of activity in the everyday life of British cities. The precinct venues were literally hidden, in the sense that they were located underground and out of sight from street level.

Making music and making change: retail developments and urban regeneration

Yet, while emphasizing the agency of musicians and their production and characterization of urban space, it is important to consider how their engagement with the physical urban environment is at the same time constrained and regulated. Music makers help to create the musical landscapes that characterize physical urban environments but they are in turn characterized by those environments. This is illustrated by the following discussion, which uses the case of St Johns precinct to consider how music making has been affected by physical urban regeneration initiatives. We begin by going further back in time than the 1970s, to the opening of the old St Johns market, in order to situate the precinct and its pubs within a context of urban change and development and to consider the development, through urbanization, of a symbiotic relationship between retail developments and live music performance.

A synergy of entertainment and retail: St Johns market and precinct

St Johns precinct replaced the old St Johns market, which was built in 1822. During the nineteenth century, most provincial British towns and cities built at least one municipal market hall but St Johns market was the first grand covered market hall in Britain. As such, it was innovative and has been described as a precursor of the modern indoor shopping precinct.[6] It was made of stone and brick with a wealth of windows and gas lights; it incorporated a large central space used for social, public and musical events and was flanked by avenues lined with stalls. It was built in response to the rapid pace of urbanization in Liverpool, and the need to provide a more effective means of marketing food and other goods to a growing urban population. A centralized, enclosed market hall was also a way for the authorities to assert social control and block urban sprawl. The market was built in the middle of three city squares – Clayton, Williamson and Queen Squares – but some distance from the old town centre. It was located in a derelict space formerly used for rope making, which lay adjacent to central entertainment establishments (including a circus,[7] two grand theatres[8] and a music hall[9]) and the city's main railway station, which eventually opened in 1833. From the beginning, therefore, the market was closely connected to live music performance and other forms of entertainment. Saturday night at the market became a popular working-class occasion and the presence of the market encouraged the further development of entertainment and retail within the area. In fact, one 1875 map[10] of public houses shows that there were sixty-eight pubs within a hundred yards of the market.

Consequently, the area became a hangout for market-goers, theatrical types and visiting seafarers, and a focal point for underground gay activity. Unsurprisingly, perhaps, it did not have a great reputation among the city's upper classes. Yet the market, with its planned combination of leisure and retail, helped to make the area the new commercial heart of the city and a local landmark, hence Clayton Square is mentioned in the lyrics for two Liverpool folk songs and a 1960s 'beat' group named themselves the Clayton Squares.

Many of the area's theatres and restaurants had been replaced from the 1920s by penny arcades and cheap movie theatres. During the Second World War, like other parts of Liverpool, it was badly damaged by enemy air-raids. As St Johns market was left to deteriorate to the point of being a health hazard, the area became further devalued, so in 1962 it became the focus of a large, ambitious scheme to redesign and rebuild Liverpool city centre. The scheme involved tackling bomb damage, knocking down city-centre slums and moving the residents to new estates on the city outskirts. It also involved initiatives designed to encourage economic growth and investment, given the decline in port activity and the fact that local unemployment was twice the national average. The flagship of this redevelopment scheme was St Johns precinct, which replaced the old market and represented a modernist, planned, managed and integrated response to leisure and retail provision.

By building the precinct, Liverpool city council aimed to rationalize the use of space and eradicate what the plan referred to as 'non-conformist' use of the area.[11] The council had extensive ownership of land and property in and around the area, which was transferred to a single private property developer. This corporation was to build what was described as 'the biggest pedestrianized shopping precinct in Europe' (*Guardian*, 21 September 1962), a 'glittering and sophisticated environment for shopping' (*Liverpool Echo*, 20 September 1962). Much like US suburban shopping centres of earlier decades, the precinct was envisaged as 'a unified civic, social and shopping centre' and 'a new miniature town in the centre of the city' (*Liverpool Daily Post*, 9 April 1970). It would occupy several levels and incorporate water gardens, a multi-storey car park, a hotel and ballroom, a new retail market to replace the existing St Johns market, and several licensed premises, including the basement pubs and a tower with a revolving restaurant and bar. There would be subways leading to the precinct from the main railway station as well as pedestrian footbridges, subways and escalators from street level. New transport networks were also developed, including new ring roads to bring goods and people to the precinct and on through the city centre.

Existing shops and family-owned businesses were demolished to make way for the new precinct, as were cinemas and theatres, the old St Johns market, and numerous pubs. By the time the precinct finally opened in 1971, however, Liverpool's economic problems had worsened and it was reported in the local newspapers that 75 per cent of the precinct's retail spaces remained vacant. In addition, many loyal customers of the old market had been displaced from the city centre as part of the postwar slum clearance and were no longer shopping in the area. It wasn't long before the precinct was being described in the local media as a planning disaster and as 'bleak', 'gloomy', 'depressing' and 'claustrophobic' (*Liverpool Daily Post*, 8 August 1975). Some historians have described it as a 'dead urban heartland', along with similar shopping precincts in Manchester and Birmingham (Carls and Schmiechen 1999: 213). Yet for the musicians we interviewed, the precinct basement was, for a time, very much alive, a unique musical and creative space that provided an opportunity for public performance at a time when such opportunities were disappearing from the city centre.

Shifting landscapes of music and retail: Clayton Square and Liverpool One

The St Johns market and precinct thus help to illustrate how local music making is shaped and regulated by urban planning and regeneration, and to highlight interconnections between shifting landscapes of music and retail. So why did the precinct's music venues disappear? Again, international trends in indoor shopping provide one possible explanation. While leisure and entertainment might have been regarded as a means of attracting shoppers and their spending to retail developments, during the 1970s and 1980s the emphasis shifted towards shopping, with leisure and entertainment regarded as a distraction from the purchase of goods. The Clayton Square shopping 'centre', for example, was built right next to St Johns precinct in the mid-1980s, just around the time when the precinct pubs closed. Its design illustrated a new trend towards indoor shopping 'centres' made of glass in order to allow for natural lighting, and a new focus on keeping customers moving around the shops. Thus, in contrast to St Johns, the Clayton Square centre had no restaurants, pubs or seating, and was more highly policed and monitored. It was also closed in the evenings, blocking off what had once been a central public space and thoroughfare. It was therefore a focus for public critique and expressions of loss. During the 1990s, for example, an 'alternative' rock band from Liverpool named Shack released a song entitled 'Who Killed Clayton Square?' 'Clayton Square', explained one of the band's members, 'was like where the gay community lived. Now it's been demolished, just like that; taken out of the city and replaced with a new shopping centre. Clayton Square was beautiful.'[12]

During the 1990s, however, Clayton Square and other retail outlets in Liverpool city centre had to compete with the emergence of new suburban shopping centres. They included industrial shopping estates but also mega indoor shopping centres such as the Trafford Centre near Manchester, which has restaurants, cinemas and other forms of entertainment. Partly in response to this, there was renewed emphasis on retail development within Liverpool city centre, and a return to a planned combination of retail and leisure. Forty-two acres of land were redeveloped to create a new billion-pound regeneration scheme, Liverpool One, described by policy makers as 'Europe's biggest shopping development' and as 'key to Liverpool's remarkable renaissance'.[13] The project involved the transfer of council land to one private property developer. It was to see a combination of themed shopping zones; walkways and footbridges; cafés, restaurants and cinemas; a street market; an underground car park; new transport links; and late-night opening. The development became the new heart of Liverpool city centre, making the St Johns and Clayton Square shopping centres more marginal. The future of St Johns precinct thus re-emerged as a topic for debate. Moreover, parts of the precinct were officially deemed a public eyesore and were temporarily covered up as part of preparations for Liverpool's ECoC year.

The St Johns market and precinct and the Liverpool One development are significantly different but all involve a planned, integrated mix of retail and leisure, and have been envisaged as tourist attractions and as a means of reshaping Liverpool city centre. In addition, the precinct and Liverpool One developments illustrate how Liverpool and other port and industrial cities have been remodelled as part of a wider process of social and economic restructuring, and rebranded as centres of consumption. Among other things, this has involved attracting corporate capital investment, thus increasing the privatization of urban space and corporate influence on the urban night-time economy. Musicians, along with other city residents, have had to grapple with the implications and effects of such policies. In Liverpool, they have often situated music within a heightened politics of culture and space. A high-profile campaign was fought, for example, to save one music-related site from demolition for the Liverpool One development[14] but what further impact will this development have on local music making? The case of St Johns precinct suggests that the current transformation of UK urban environments into centres for shopping and consumption has implications for music making, and it raises questions about shopping centres as artistic or creative environments.

Music, heritage and urban regeneration

The case of St Johns precinct and its rock pubs can also help to relate music making to a politics of heritage and regeneration. Over the past few decades there has been increasing emphasis in the UK, Europe and North America on urban regeneration not just through retail but also through culture. Culture has been used, among other things, to promote cities as distinctive places so that they can compete for visitors and investment (Robins 1991). This has involved the development of local cultural tourism and heritage, and the re-imaging of cities through competitions such as the European Capital of Culture. Inevitably, this raises familiar questions: Whose culture? Whose heritage?

In Liverpool, public and private sector organizations have transformed certain sites of musical significance into heritage sites, constructing a dominant tourist landscape based on music. So far, the focus has been on the Beatles, the Cavern Club and the 1960s Merseybeat scene, but recently attention has also turned to Liverpool's post-punk scene of the early 1980s, associated with bands such as Echo and the Bunnymen and a club called Eric's (see chapter 7). The precinct pubs, along with countless other local venues, have not yet been a focus for official constructions of local music heritage. Paul Du Noyer certainly has little to say about them, or about the 1970s more generally, in his book on the history of Liverpool popular music, which was recently republished to mark the city's ECoC celebrations. The only 1970s band to get a mention there is Supercharge, but that group is described as 'the tail-end of a previous generation and not the start of a new one' (Du Noyer 2007: 103).

The precinct venues could be described as a hidden history – hidden between Liverpool's 'Merseybeat' and post-punk scenes. The 1970s emerge as a fallow period in constructions of Liverpool's popular music, a period when there was 'nothing going on' and 'nothing much happened', while in terms of the history of popular music more generally the music scholar Andy Bennett (2007) describes the 1970s as 'the forgotten decade'. This may help to explain why some of the musicians we spoke to appeared cautious when assessing the significance of the precinct, and described its pub scene as over-shadowed and threatened by the trend to discotheques in the early to mid-1970s – which meant that fewer venues booked live musicians – and by the arrival and notoriety of punk later in that decade.

Nevertheless, one musician who performed at the Moonstone has produced a self-published book on 1970s Liverpool music entitled *Plug Inn (The Forgotten Years)* (Bolland 2006). He has also organized reunion performances and produced a website targeted at the musicians he hung out with during that time.[15] He described the Moonstone to us as 'a great place to be, and so exciting – "the forgotten years" – such an exciting time and yet no one ever talks about it'. Culture-led urban regeneration has thus influenced the characterization of music and music venues as local 'heritage', and provoked the construction of alternative and contested music heritages.

Conclusion

The pub rock venues of St Johns precinct had all disappeared by the late 1980s and were converted into retail storage spaces, while the Top Rank Suite ballroom was demolished to make room for additional car parking. There is almost no trace of these venues within Liverpool's contemporary urban landscape. Similarly, there is very little recognition of the broader era of music making in Liverpool during the 1970s in historical accounts of the city. In this chapter we have described these venues through the memories of some of the many musicians who performed in them. Their accounts help to illustrate how music making characterizes physical urban environments. By situating the precinct and its pubs within a wider context of urban planning and development, we have pointed out that music making is at the same time characterized by those environments and the regeneration initiatives through which they are transformed and regulated, and implicated within a politics of culture, space and heritage.

Acknowledgements

The research for this chapter was conducted as part of a project funded by the UK Arts and Humanities Research Council (AHRC, Landscape and Environment programme) in partnership with English Heritage and National Museums Liverpool. We would like to thank the AHRC and our partner organizations for their contribution to and support for the project.

Notes

1 Including £6 billion investment across the city, spearheaded by the £1 billion 'Liverpool One' retail development in the city centre (information taken from www.bigdig.liverpool.gov.uk, no longer live).
2 'Trog oil' is a colloquial name for patchouli oil, an essential oil popular from the 1960s as the perfume of choice for many hippies and rock fans.
3 Moonstone patron commenting on the Yo! Liverpool community web forum under the string 'Legendary Liverpool Clubs of Yesteryear', at www.yoliverpool.com (accessed 20 October 2008).
4 Birkenhead lies across the River Mersey from Liverpool on the Wirral peninsula.
5 Cover bands are groups that typically play well known songs written by other artists.
6 Information from www.buildinghistory.org/Buildings/Markethalls.htm (accessed February 2008).
7 The Philip Astley's circus, established at Christian Street in 1789, which became the Olympic Circus in 1805.
8 Theatre Royal built in 1772 (rebuilt as the Royal Court), and the new Adelphi theatre, built in 1803.
9 The Star music hall (which became the Playhouse).
10 *Comparative Frontages of Public Houses and Private Houses, &c,* 1875, located at Liverpool Record Office, Hq647 94SMY.
11 City Centre Planning Group, 1965, cited in Deller and Ryan (2007: 17).
12 Quote taken from www.shacknet.co.uk/interviews-shack-sounds-03-88.htm (accessed March, 2005), cited in Cohen (2007).
13 Quotes taken from www.liverpoolpsda.co.uk (accessed February 2008).
14 Gibson and Homan (2004: 74) illustrate the negative consequences of similar developments for landmark music venues in Sydney, while Chatterton and Hollands (2003) and Jones and Wilks-Heeg (2004) highlight the threat that they pose to 'alternative' music culture in British cities.
15 Pluginn (The Forgotten Years) website, www.pluginn.bravehost.com (accessed June 2010).

References

Bennett, Andy (2007) 'The Forgotten Decade: Rethinking the Popular Music of the 1970s'. *Popular Music History* 2(1): 5–24.
Bolland, Tony (2006) *Plug Inn (The Forgotten Years).* Liverpool: Bolland and Lowe.
Carls, Kenneth and James Schmiechen (1999) *The British Markethall: A Social and Architectural History.* New Haven, CT: Yale University Press.

Chatterton, Paul and Robert Hollands (2003) *Urban Nightscapes: Youth Cultures, Pleasure Spaces and Corporate Power*. London: Routledge.

Cohen, Sara (2007) *Decline, Renewal and the City in Popular Music Culture: Beyond the Beatles*. Aldershot: Ashgate.

Deller, Jeremy and Paul Ryan (2007) *The Liverpool of Brian Epstein*. Liverpool: Tate Liverpool. Also www.jeremydeller.org/epstein/index.htm (accessed October 2008).

Du Noyer, Paul (2007) *Liverpool: Wondrous Place – Music from the Cavern to the Capital of Culture*. London: Virgin.

Finnegan, Ruth (1989) *The Hidden Musicians: Music-Making in an English Town*. Cambridge: Cambridge University Press.

Gibson, Chris and Shane Homan (2004) 'Urban Redevelopment, Live Music and Public Space: Cultural Performance and the Re-Making of Marrickville'. *International Journal of Cultural Policy* 10(1): 67–84.

Jones, Paul and Stuart Wilks-Heeg (2004) 'Capitalising Culture: Liverpool 2008'. *Local Economy* 19(4): 341–60.

Moore, Alan (2006) 'What Story Should a History of Popular Music Tell?' *Popular Music History* 1(3): 329–38.

Robins, K. (1991) 'Traditions and Translation: National Culture in Its Global Context'. In: John Corner and Sylvia Harvey (eds) *Enterprise and Heritage: Crosscurrents of National Culture*. London: Routledge. pp. 21–44.

CHAPTER 5

The soul continuum: Liverpool black musicians and the UK music industry from the 1950s to the 1980s

Robert Strachan

Introduction

This chapter examines the history of music making among Liverpool's black communities since the late 1950s. It uses oral histories provided by musicians, music industry workers and prominent community figures to draw out key issues relating to a significant narrative in Liverpool's musical history. In addition, it examines the way in which Liverpool artists have had an affinity with African-American musical forms such as doo-wop and soul. It argues that the predominance of vocal harmony groups in the history of black music in the city can be understood as a direct reflection of the unique experience of Liverpool's black communities. The fact that Liverpool's black population was established before those in most other British cities (with very specific patterns of migration) resulted in a specific set of musical practices that have hitherto been ignored in histories of British black music. Indeed, this particular set of conditions means that the experience of Liverpool musicians constitutes an early and important facet of the history of black music in the UK.

As various scholars have noted (Christian 1998, 2000; Small 2002; Bolland 2010), any discussion of 'black identity'[1] within the city is complex and the use of the terms 'black communities' and 'black music' within this chapter does not seek to obscure the diverse nature of experience, ethnicity and migration, or the multitude of differing historical narratives that these factors might engender. Rather, these terms are deployed here in order to explore commonalities within the lived experience of the musicians under discussion and the way in which ethnicity and culture have had real and material effects in terms of their musical experiences within Liverpool and their trajectory within the British recording industry from the 1960s onwards.

Historiography

The specificities of black music in Liverpool raise important historio-graphical issues (that is, how the history of popular music has been written and understood) on both a local and a wider level. Both the way in which Liverpool music has been historically understood and the predominance of certain narratives in the history of UK black music have meant that the contribution of the Liverpool artists discussed here has remained relatively hidden. Black music in the city has had to contend with a highly pervasive set of dominant historical narratives. The phenomenal worldwide success of the Beatles has had a fundamental impact upon how Liverpool music has been histori-cized. The tendency of critics and commentators to tie the rise of the Beatles firmly to the city and its specific musical scenes has meant that there has been a concentration on white guitar-based groups in the construction of Liverpool's ongoing musical heritage. Specifically, Merseybeat has become *the* foundational narrative within the city's musical history, through which all subsequent developments tend to be refracted. This has meant that, on the one hand, black musicians have been seen as something of an anomalous footnote. For example, Paul Du Noyer's history of Liverpool music, *Wondrous Place*, gives just half a page to the Real Thing (Du Noyer 2002: 104), despite that group's place as the most commercially successful Liverpool band of the 1970s. On the other hand, the dominance of Merseybeat in historical accounts has resulted in a revisionist tendency whereby black artists and clubs are reclaimed as playing a central role in the development either of the Beatles or of Merseybeat as a whole.[2]

It is clear that black culture in Liverpool did indeed intersect with, and exert an influence on, Merseybeat. McGrath's (2010) research, for example, notes the contributions of black Liverpool musicians such as Vinnie Tow, Gerry Gobin and Lord Woodbine to the Beatles' musical education. However, the oral histories presented here uncover narratives which are important in their own right. First, they uncover a rich hidden history of culture within the city which illustrates how particular social and geographical factors converged to result in a specific strain of musical expression. Secondly, the story of the black music tradition in Liverpool is significant in terms of the wider development of black music in the UK and the position of black artists within the UK recording industry. Musicians such as Derry Wilkie and the Chants were some of the first post-rock-and-roll black acts to be signed to major recording companies in Britain and their stories provide an insight into the workings of the UK recording industry and media of the period.

These early artists are significant, then, in that they uncover a different story of black music in Britain, one which has been under-played in previous critical and historical work. Studies of black music in Britain have tended to focus upon musical forms associated with post-*Windrush* migration.[3] As a result, British black music has often been characterized as being expressive of African-Caribbean identities (Chambers 1985; Hebdige 1987; Oliver 1990; Back 1996; Gilroy 1997). Hence, such work often concentrates on reggae and hybrid forms which incorporate elements of Caribbean music to create particular locally based urban sounds (Hesmondhalgh and Melville 2001; Webb 2007). Because of Liverpool's particular history of migration and community, black musicians from the city do not particularly fit with this dominant narrative. Nevertheless, it is precisely because of the specificities of the Liverpool black experience that the city's artists can be seen as significant in the history of an understudied yet important facet of music making in the UK: that is, black British soul. This chapter concentrates on the soul tradition from a group of vocal acts that emerged in the city in the 1950s through to the 1980s.

Black settlement

First, it is necessary to contextualize these post-rock-and-roll musicians within a longer history of migration. People of African origin have long had a presence in the city and Liverpool's black communities have played an important part in the city's culture. Along with other British seaports such as Bristol and Cardiff, the city was among the first to develop a black presence, during the era of the European slave trade of the eighteenth and nineteenth centuries (Christian 2002: 70). The nineteenth-century settlement of black seamen in the city, who were primarily employed as cheap labour with the Elder Dempster shipping company from the 1830s (Christian 1998: 293), saw the development of an established black population. The particular West African roots of this early population has had a long-lasting effect both on local culture and on notions of 'black identity' within the city. As Nassy Brown (1998: 299) notes, 'Although there are other migration histories that account for the black presence in that city, the dominant narrative centres on these African seamen, whom black Liverpudlians commonly represented as the founding fathers of what has become the black community'.

This history has also been one of marginalization, as the black population have experienced considerable racism. As Christian (1998: 303) notes, the 'black presence in Liverpool has a long history that has been characterized by the concomitant struggle against white racism. For generations, the black community has faced an onslaught of both individual and institutionalized forms of racial oppression.' The overt racism within many white areas of the city (see Small 2002: 181) resulted in the black population being predominantly concentrated in the south end of the city and the Toxteth/Granby area in particular (often referred to as Liverpool 8, or L8, on account of its postcode, or informally as simply 'the area'). The racism experienced by many in the city centre and beyond meant that the L8 area served as both a social and an economic centre. A 1968 report noted that many black youths 'met discrimination in employment, and when they move outside [the area] ... they feel insecure' and that there was widespread 'evidence of hostility to [people of] colour in white downtown areas' of the city (Wood and Downing, cited in Hiro 1971: 251).

This exclusion meant that a distinct set of social practices developed in the Liverpool 8 area. The racism evident in the door and booking policies of city-centre clubs led to the emergence of a social scene based around the Toxteth/Granby neighbourhood. A whole network of clubs existed from the 1930s to the 1970s concentrated around Princes Avenue (one of the main thoroughfares of the

L8 area). Nigerian-born community leader Chief Angus Chukuemeka recalls a circuit of clubs in the area that included:

> the Europa club, the Gala club, the Federa … so the whole area on a Saturday was wonderful, vibrant. Of course if you went to Granby Street on Saturdays it was as if you were in one of the African cities.

In addition, participants in Martelli's (2006) ethnographic study of black music in the city remembered a series of after-hours basement clubs, such as the Mayfair, Flamingo, Palm Cove and Dutch Eddie's, where local acts would perform.

These specific social and historical contexts have had particular implications for the development of black music in the city. By the late 1950s, Liverpool had a generation of black British-born musicians and singers who had grown up in the city and were steeped in a local cultural scene where music had been central through a number of African churches and social clubs. The musicians who went on to be involved in Liverpool soul bands also had a number of role models (and in many cases family members – see Cohen and McManus 1991) among the musicians who had made their names within the Liverpool 8 area in the 1940s and early 1950s. Singers and guitarists such as Powie and Johnny Wenton (Cohen and McManus 1991: 32), Jimmy Cole, Tommy Bassett, Eddie Hamilton, Robert Amoo, Ownie and Joey Cole, and drummers such as Sammy Scotland and 'Tucker' Tagoe, had been regulars in the cellar clubs located around the Princes Avenue area (Martelli 2006: 3).[4] These social spaces were often instrumental in providing a platform for expressions of cultural identity and fostering a sense of community. For example, Chief Angus Chukuemeka commented that the African social clubs in the city were pivotal in his integration into the community when he arrived in Liverpool in the 1960s. He commented:

> there was a community that existed here since [before] 1935 so when you are a new person they do welcome you. They do make you comfortable because they know that when you are new that things will be different. They will make you feel at home…. When I started mixing up with people in the area they introduced me to these clubs and of course I found them really exciting. There was a lot of the African-American music and people would dance.

Black Liverpool and black America

Chief Chukuemeka's comments also highlight another striking implication of these particular social contexts: the way in which black Liverpool musicians have consistently drawn upon African-American music, as opposed to the more clearly African-Carribean traditions common to other British cities, such as Birmingham, London and Bristol. This is perhaps because Liverpool already had an established community of people of African descent before the 1950s and the because it did not see the scale of post-*Windrush* migration from the former British colonies that was common in other cities. There was also the fact that African-Americans had had considerable social interaction in the city with black servicemen from the racially segregated airbase at Burtonwood,[5] who often sought out entertainment in clubs in the Granby/Toxteth area.

In her ethnographic work on the relationships between black Liverpool and black America, Nassy Brown (2006) argues that while Liverpool's black population have had something of a historical ambivalence to US black culture and visiting African-Americans (in terms of class and gender), imported black American music was a real source of identification for black Liverpudlians and was a constant in the community's social life. One of her respondents commented:

> In some instances, fathers and uncles had been over to America as seamen and had brought records back. So within the black community of Liverpool we've always grown up with a type of traditional black music. If it wasn't African, it would be American – it wouldn't be so much West Indian, Caribbean music around that time. (Nassy Brown 1998: 303)

Similarly, Jenkins (1994) pointed to the existence of cellar parties and blues clubs as early as the 1930s where guitar groups would often play improvised sets of 'half African' and half African-American music (quoted in Brocken 2010: 50). This is not to say that there was a complete lack of Caribbean influence on the city's music scene. Indeed, Trinidad-born band leader and club owner Lord Woodbine was actually one of the 500 West Indians to arrive in England aboard the *Empire Windrush* in June 1948. Many of Cohen's (2007: 21) respondents in her ethnographic study of popular music in the city also remembered calypso and mento being performed in Liverpool during the 1940s and 1950s.

Nevertheless, it is the influence of US styles such as R&B, doo-wop and soul that have had a long-standing influence on black musicians in the city. In the late 1950s and 1960s a number of black artists emerged such as Sugar Deen and Colin Areety, the Earls, the Sobells, the Challengers, the Conquests, the Poppies, the Shuffler Sound/ Buzz Brothers and the Chants; they all came from the Liverpool 8 area and shared an affinity with the black American vocal groups that were popular in the UK in the 1950s. For many local musicians, the emergence of American doo-wop (and later soul music) chimed with existing musical practices within the city. Both Joe Ankrah (of the Chants) and Sugar Deen (of the Earls, Valentinos and Harlems) recall hearing US acts such as Frankie Lymon and the Teenagers and suggested they were pivotal to their engagement with music. These American artists provided both a set of role models for young black musicians in the city and (in some cases) a point of stylistic identification that chimed with their formative musical experiences through the church.

> JOE ANKRAH: I was working in Art Craft as a commercial artist: we were doing posters for the Empire Theatre and I delivered them. One day when I was coming out of the Empire box office I got mobbed by a gang of girls and they were going 'Oh there he is, come on!' and I discovered that these girls thought that I was a singer called Frankie Lymon. Frankie Lymon was a young black American guy who was about 15 with his brothers; there was about five of them all together, and they were a vocal group and they made just vocal songs which I find fantastic, you know, just have a bass singer. One of the songs I remember them doing was 'Why Do Fools Fall in Love?' [a UK number one in 1956] and it used to start with a bassline going, then all the harmonies used to come and I remembered that from all the time and I had all this going on in my head and I used to think to myself 'All I need is, like, another four people and we could be in show business', you know, 'cause I didn't even think I couldn't sing: I just knew I could sing. I had been singing all my life in church.

> SUGAR DEEN: Because I was always into harmonies when the likes of Frankie Lymon and the Teenagers came out I thought, that is what I want to do. It was just all about harmonies. It wasn't so much as the lead vocal voice – it was the harmonies where they were arranged around the vocals and I thought, yeah, that is my bag. So that was my influences and, of course, we were getting stuff like the Drifters and

the early days coming through; I think before that as a kid was the Mills Brothers and that was the early fifties. I used to listen that stuff, the harmonies, so they were my main influences basically.

Thus, the influence of these US groups provided a point of identification for young black musicians in the city, in that the foregrounding of vocal harmony in doo-wop constituted a popular manifestation of practices that had been part of their formative musical experiences. In addition, the popular mythology of doo-wop as a social practice was easily integrated into the everyday lives of these singers. In popular accounts, US doo-wop acts were often positioned through a romantic representation of street singing. This framing, along with the fact that the performance of vocal harmony tunes did not need any specific technology or expensive equipment, meant that street singing became a common practice, one which could be undertaken within the singers' neighbourhoods as a form of public display and a source of social affirmation:

EDDIE AMOO: I've always been heavily into ... doo-wop ... [it's] the type of thing that you can sing walking round the streets ... with your mates. Even if you're not actually singing the harmonies you can mimic what you're listening to on records ... and that's what me and my mates used to do. We'd have a Miracles' song or the Drifters, the Del Vikings' 'Come Go With Me', and we used to walk round the streets singing all of this. We'd all end up on the same part but we used to have fun you know, and it gradually developed from that.

JOE ANKRAH: If we went out with our mates we would get on corners, street corners and we would sing. We liked the attention that the singing attracted, you know, because all of a sudden people were taking notice of us. I suppose we were all frustrated screaming out for attention really: 'Look at me. I'm here. I am alive.' I suppose that is what it was all about.

SUGAR DEEN: [In the late 1950s] Tony Fail ... sang with me and a couple of others. He lived in Kent Gardens, which is a little bit further down from where I lived in St James' Gardens, and they had a big archway there and we used to sing in the archway; the acoustics were brilliant so we used to rehearse in that archway of the block and especially on a summer night you get people on the landings and they would be listening and then they would be shouting down requests: 'Sing blah, blah', 'Can you sing so and so?' Everyone seemed to love it in the blocks.

GEORGE DIXON, OF THE BAND THE IN CROWD: Oh it was, it was the harmonies [that I loved about soul music]. It was such a big thing;

mostly a lot of falsetto you know. I can't do it now but really, falsetto behind all the vocals and it brought all the vocals together. So, no matter what soul songs we did, there was just a big vocal going on there. I formed another band which was called Just Us and that was two black guys, me and a fella called Willy Wenton … and that was a fantastic vocal band you know.

This historical identification with US black music can be seen as in keeping with patterns in the travel and hybridization of different musical forms. Paul Gilroy (1996, 1997), for instance, provides a useful theorization of the way in which black music travels around the diaspora on overlapping and complex routes, following a variety of directions. Gilroy describes how many different forms of black music share formal characteristics across geographical locations. In Gilroy's theorization this is not indicative of any core essence of black music *per se* but, rather, indicates that differing communities of the African diaspora share certain experiences and thus identify with and adapt what he calls 'black expressive cultural forms' (Gilroy 1996). Rather than constituting a linear and unbroken progression of musical forms directly from a singular African route, musicians absorb influences from music of the African diaspora (through factors such as media and travel) and mix and adapt them to local contexts (and, indeed, mix them with other globalized musical forms).

For many of Liverpool's black musicians, then, African-American musical forms mediated through radio, film and recordings made sense in the context of their lived experience of the city. Their use and adaptation of US vocal harmonies was at the same time expressive of local identities and a positioning of what it meant to be black in Britain at that time within a wider, international nexus of black experience. This complex mapping of identities through a combination of mediated musical forms and a highly specific local culture is somewhat different to the way in which black music in Britain has been characterized in many historical narratives. Often, patterns of immigration (particularly from the West Indies) have been seen as the major conduit for diasporic musical forms. The example of Liverpool musicians actually serves to problematize this narrative, by illustrating how a differing set of routes and roots (Gilroy 1996) had a profound effect upon a significant group of musicians in British black music history.

British black music and the music industry

Liverpool's particular social context provided a cultural milieu which allowed a home-grown black music scene to develop significantly before, and in a different way to, that in other British cities. However, despite the worldwide fame of Liverpool as a musical centre in the early and mid-1960s and the international success of several Merseybeat acts, commercial success eluded a whole generation of black artists from the city. This is despite the fact that many acts were contemporaneous with bands such as the Beatles, Gerry and the Pacemakers and the Searchers, and were often connected with the Merseybeat scene. Indeed, Derry Wilkie's Seniors were the first Liverpool band to be given a Hamburg residency, in 1960, a route that the Beatles and many others were to follow. According to Clayson (1997: 68) the Seniors' first Hamburg booking was hastily arranged, after a residency in Blackpool for the band had been cancelled by Larry Parnes, perhaps the most important pop music impresario of the time. The band went on to be the first Merseybeat act to record for a major label, Fontana, which released their *Twist At the Top* album in February 1962 (released under the name of Howie Casey and the Seniors). Wilkie's experience with a major label illustrates that recording companies were more than willing to sign acts from the region, irrespective of race. Indeed, several other black Liverpool musicians gained record deals at around the same time. The Chants went through a series of major label deals in the 1960s, initially signing with PYE in 1963 before recording releases for Fontana, Decca, Larry Page's Page One records, and RCA; Steve Aldo signed a solo deal with Decca in 1964 and worked with EMI two years later; while Sugar Deen's bands the Ramones and the Harlems both had ill fated spells with EMI and DJM (Dick James's record label), respectively.

How, then, do we account for the relative obscurity of these Liverpool soul acts and their failure to gain critical and commercial success, even though they had been integrated into the recording industry at a relatively early stage? Perhaps an easy suggestion to make would be that this was the result of a pervading racism in the music industry. However, while the music industry doubtless was reflective of the society in which it existed, the deliberate blocking of the promotion of (their own) black artists would seem self-defeating on the part of recording companies. Indeed, UK labels had backed a number (albeit small) of (predominantly London-based) black British artists in the years that immediately preceded the beat explosion. The Southlanders had experienced some success with Decca (including the top ten single 'Alone' in 1957), while Neville Taylor and the Cutters had been signed to Parlophone in the late 1950s and had appeared on the television music show *Oh Boy!* a number of times during this period. In addition, London-born black British singer/songwriter Kenny Lynch[6] had a number of UK hits throughout the early 1960s with a series of lushly orchestrated pop tunes and slickly produced cover versions of US hits such as Goffin and King's 'Up on the Roof'[7] and Cardiff-born Shirley Bassey had a number of chart entries from 1959 onwards.

Rather than overt racism as a singular causal factor, one can perhaps point to a combination of factors related to the way in which the British music industry operated at the time in terms of its marketing strategies and promotion of particular musical styles. Hence, it is necessary to examine how these acts intersected with the dominant practices of the recording industry at that particular historical moment. A major factor here concerns musical style. If one examines the UK charts during the period 1963–65 one can identify a number of dominant styles which were championed by the recording and media industries: British beat music, home-grown pop (often solo singers performing Brill Building-style numbers, backed by session musicians and orchestral arrangements), easy listening, US pop artists and a smattering of US soul and Motown. Black Liverpool acts did not necessarily fit in with the musical styles which were being prioritized by the UK recording industry from 1963 onwards. The dynamic soul of Steve Aldo's releases, Derry Wilkie's R&B vocal stylings and the vocal harmonies of the Chants and the Valentinos were neither beat nor straight pop and, crucially, they were British at a time when soul was understood as an American form. Al Peters, who recorded demos for major labels with Colin Areety and the multi-racial Liverpool R&B group the Almost Blues (whose line-up included singers Eddie Williams and Tommy Browne), notes that the recording industry didn't want R&B groups from Liverpool, as it didn't fit the stereotype (quoted in Brocken 2010: 147).

Other black British artists, such as Lynch and Bassey, already had a musical context in terms of production and marketplace that the Liverpool acts did not. As Eddie Amoo (of the Chants and later the Real Thing) notes, producers and 'artists and repertoire' (A&R) personnel sometimes attempted during the recording process to try to adapt the sound of vocal groups into a style which was perhaps inappropriate:

> Most black bands in this country that were recorded were recorded like white bands, and they sounded like white bands. They used to record the Chants like a white pop band, which we weren't. We weren't musically adept enough in them days to establish what we really wanted ourselves – we weren't musicians then.[8]

Steve Higginson draws on this evidence to argue that:

> the real reasons why Derry Wilkie, the Chants, the Valentinos, Steve Aldo et al did not gain far greater reward that their talents merited was simply because their style and aesthetic ran contrary to the music business and the musical forms of the day. We had local talent who themselves were fusing gospel, a cappella, and producing driving R&B when the overall musical culture of the UK was narrow and insular.[9]

Ironically, then, it was perhaps their grounding in US musical forms that may have been an obstacle to Liverpool acts achieving commercial success. Nowhere is this more pertinent than in terms of marketing. Black musicians from Liverpool had to compete in a market where, by the mid-1960s, American soul records were being licensed by the UK arms of major labels and smaller independents. In this context, black music, and soul in particular, tended to be framed and marketed as American. It is perhaps significant that the handful of notably successful British-based black R&B and soul singers of the period were born outside the UK: Geno Washington was a US-born ex-serviceman who had been stationed in the UK; Jimmy James was already a successful singer in Jamaica before he and his band moved to the UK in 1964; and P. P. Arnold was 'discovered' by the Rolling Stones singing for Ike and Tina Turner's soul review in the US and brought to the UK to record with Andrew Loog Oldham's Immediate label.

There is some evidence to suggest that the marketing departments of recording companies did not know how to successfully promote black British acts owing to the predominance of US acts in this particular sector of the market. As Eddie Amoo reflected, 'the Chants were "raw", uncommercial (for the time), and above all, black. PYE had no idea how to market them' (quoted in Martelli 2006: 9). This lack of understanding was perhaps a result of how the UK music industry launched and marketed acts at this time, specifically their reliance upon television as a promotional medium. A series of television pop shows in the late 1950s was crucial to the emergence of a distinct British pop industry. By 1957 the BBC television pop show *Six-Five Special* was regularly attracting audiences of over six million. The series was instrumental in launching the careers of British pop performers such as Adam Faith, Terry Dene and Marty Wilde, all of whom had chart hits on the back of appearances on the show. The success of the series was followed by a series of British television shows which became central in the marketing of pop acts throughout the 1960s. It has been noted that British music television was somewhat resistant to black music *per se*,[10] but the exclusion of these Liverpool acts seems to have resulted more from the assumption that black musical forms were performed by black American musicians:

> JOE ANKRAH: I remember us doing two television shows in one week [with] the Chants and we had another one coming up on the Saturday, which they cancelled. The manager went 'Well what is going down?' you know? They said 'Oh we only have two American acts on a week on TV' and the manager turned round and said 'Well my boys are not American they are from England'. But the point was made: if you were black you were American, you know, end of story. So that was it; so that was something in your face.

> SUGAR DEEN: [We] read in the paper that they were having auditions [for] ... *Round the Country*. It was a talent thing and it would be on the radio, so you go along and audition which [in Liverpool] was [at] the Empire. In them days nobody really wanted to know a black performer, black acts and that kind of R&B-type British black acts. There was just no interest so you would go on there and you would strut your stuff and then a little girl would come on, a little tutu, little fairy dress, you know, little blonde, blue-eyed girl, pretty, singing 'The Good Ship Lollipop' or something and win it and you would think 'What?' So it was that kind of thing. So nothing really ever materialized in the auditions that we did.

Clearly, this reluctance to give airtime to black British acts shows a contradictory attitude to musical appropriation that belies an undercurrent of institutionalized racism. The same programmes had no such qualms about including white British appropriations of US genres. Similarly, visiting black US acts were framed within a discourse of geographical and racial authenticity. By the time that black Liverpool acts had gained recording contracts, it was much more common for US soul acts to cross the Atlantic and appear on British pop shows. Perhaps the most important UK pop television show of the 1960s, *Ready Steady Go!*, for instance, featured appearances from Marvin Gaye, Otis Redding, the Supremes, Stevie Wonder, Smokey Robinson and Martha Reeves and the Vandellas among others during its existence between 1963 and 1966. This was in contrast to previous UK shows, such as *Six-Five Special* and *Oh Boy!*, both of which had fewer visiting US artists. Hence, it may be the case that easier access to African-American stars led to fewer black British acts appearing on UK television.

This lack of exposure meant that mainstream success within the recording industry eluded the Liverpool groups of the time. Most had to seek alternative sources of income and many Liverpool soul groups found work in the extensive national live music and cabaret circuit, which provided a steady source of employment for musicians in the UK. This was often hard work, involving long periods on the road with limited finances. As George Dixon explains:

> I did it with the In Crowd and believe you me it's really, really hard you know. People think it's so all roses but it's not. It's so hard, it really is. I mean at one time you're travelling from South Wales up to Scotland, which is a long trek, especially when the van broke down and we had to tow it up there you know. It's a long way to go.

Nevertheless, it is a testimony to the professionalism of these Liverpool acts and the adaptability of the soul vocal harmony style that many had significant success on the cabaret circuit well into the 1970s. Sugar Deen had a long career with the Valentinos during this period, while Joe and Edmund Ankrah's post-Chants outfit, Ashanti, went on to appear on ITV's *New Faces*, a variety competition which was instrumental in breaking many British cabaret acts into the British entertainment mainstream. Indeed, it was another variety talent show, *Opportunity Knocks*, which would provide the first national exposure for the Real Thing, a vocal harmony group formed by Chris Amoo in 1972.

At the same time, soul and funk continued to be at the heart of the grass-roots scene in Liverpool 8 and beyond. DJ Les Spaine (who would go on to be one of the most influential A&R staff in black British music) promoted club nights called the Pun and the Timepiece, which were among the first successful funk nights in the country. The Timepiece especially gained a national reputation, to the extent that African-American servicemen would travel to its all-nighters from all over the UK (Wilson 2004). Spaine also brought live acts such as Chairmen of the Board and the Ohio Players to the city, as well as supporting local acts such as L8 Connection (a funk, soul act that had various independent releases in the 1970s and 1980s) and the all-female L8 group Distinction. It was the Real Thing, however, that would go on to find artistic and commercial success through fusing funk, soul and disco with Liverpool's vocal tradition.

The Real Thing and Brit-soul

After a number of false starts and recording contracts which came to nothing, the Real Thing eventually signed with PYE in 1975 and went on to become the most successful UK soul group of the 1970s. While the band is perhaps most remembered for its enduring pop hits such as 'Can't Get By Without You', 'You To Me Are Everything' and 'Can You Feel the Force', it is the songwriting partnership of Eddie (who joined the band in 1975) and Chris Amoo that provided a lasting (but somewhat overlooked) legacy in the history of British black music, by spearheading a movement towards a distinctly British social commentary. As Eddie Amoo remembers:

> I started to feel that I wanted to really project what had happened to me and the people that I'd grew up with in my songs. I wanted to come up with something that would really stand up against what the Americans were doing, Curtis Mayfield and people like that. When you grow up in a place like Toxteth and you're black you grow up with a lot of different perceptions and experiences than you'd have if you were white growing up in a middle-class district. I wanted to project this and in [the] very early days of the Real Thing I wrote the song called 'Vicious Circle'. It wasn't just about the black experience [but was also] about politicians from a working-class point of view. The way politicians use the working class to move up [the social ladder] and then don't come up good on the promise[s] that they make. That's what 'Vicious Circle' was about and I started to build up from that.

This trend in the Real Thing's songwriting reached its ultimate fruition in the 1977 album *Four From Eight*, a themed collection of songs which echoed the politicized work of US artists such as Curtis Mayfield and Marvin Gaye, who, on albums such as their respective *Superfly* (1972) and *What's Going On* (1971), had started to reflect issues relevant to the African-American urban situation through a distinctly socially conscious soul music. The Amoos' innovation was to adapt these trends to reflect a particularly British and specifically Liverpudlian experience. As Eddie comments:

> We came up with a song called 'Children of the Ghetto' [which] was basically about growing up in Toxteth. We liked it so much ... that we thought, well let's write as many songs about Toxteth as we can ... [what] the Real Thing were doing, was very, very riffy, very, very musical you know, the riffs of the music were the dominant factor in the show, which was pretty new for a black group then.... In other words, we got away completely from the polished American thing and we were heading more towards like the Parliament Funkadelic type thing.... 'Children of the Ghetto' fitted into that perfectly and from that we developed songs like 'Stanhope Street'.... Stanhope Street was like a hub within Toxteth and then we came up with the song 'Liverpool 8' which ... tied the whole thing together and this eventually became the basis for our album *Four From Eight*.

By fusing funk, disco and soul to create a soundtrack to a contemporary urban theme, the band was seeking to develop its work in an overt attempt to transcend American influences. Eddie Amoo notes that *Four From Eight* was:

> absolutely [a conscious decision to reflect the British black experience] because we'd come such a long way musically and we wanted to really make it clear that we had a different thing going than the Americans. It was clear that both musically and in terms of the band's image and artwork in those days most of the black groups were modelled and marketed along the lines of [groups] like the Stylistics and people like that and we'd gone beyond that and we wanted people to really realize that, like, we were totally different and we were doing our own thing.

The band was not the first black British group to make socially conscious records (the Equals' 1967 release 'Police On My Back' was clearly influenced by the thematic realism of Jamaican ska) or to fuse funk and soul in a British context (the commercially unsuccessful but highly influential early 1970s outfit Cymande being a notable example). However, by 1977 the Real Thing was significant in an upsurge in black British music that would go on to have a considerable impact upon the commercial mainstream of the UK recording industry. The band was symptomatic of a new fusing of African-American music with an outlook rooted in black British culture and UK pop production, which would result in success for a number of home-grown soul, funk and disco groups which followed in their wake (such as Hi Tension, Linx, Imagination, Rokotto, Heatwave and the Olympic Runners). Nevertheless, the band remained a product of its formative environment and a direct line can be traced from a Liverpool tradition of vocal soul music that had existed since the 1950s. Both the personnel of the band and the foregrounding of vocal harmonies in their work firmly routed them within this tradition. Thus, the band's importance within Brit-soul and the breakthrough of black British music in the late 1970s and 1980s serves to reinforce the importance of the early Liverpool groups in a continuum of British soul music. The initial identification by Liverpool groups with black American forms in the 1950s and early 1960s established a specific and highly localized musical tradition in the city that would continue for nearly thirty years.

The fascination with the harmonies central to black US forms was to continue to have a lasting effect on Liverpool's black music. It certainly carried through to the hit 1980s group the Christians. As Garry Christian comments:

> [I started] back in 1974 with a group called Equal Temperament. My brother Rick, who is three years older than me, he is a classically trained music teacher. He teaches in schools around Liverpool to this day in fact. He is a great musician and he put us together. We called ourselves Equal Temperament. It was the worst name they could have called us really because there was no Equal Temperament at all: family, brothers, siblings, they are always fighting. They are always arguing about something. There we were and we just did the local clubs and stuff and it was mainly a cappella, singing with no music at all and that was great. He taught us how to harmonize really, how to put these noises and different tones together, so that was great. That was another learning curve for me, how to harmonize.

By the time the Christians emerged in the 1980s, the context of the music industry had shifted significantly for British black musicians. As well as the success of the Real Thing and Brit-soul, the late 1970s had seen the emergence of two connected British musical movements. First, British reggae bands had begun to emerge from the African-Carribean communities in cities such as Birmingham and London. Acts such as Steel Pulse and Aswad gained significant national and international followings. By 1979 the multiracial post-punk movement Two-Tone (named after the Coventry based independent label Two-Tone) had become something of a phenomenon in the UK recording industry. The artistic and commercial success of these British hybrid forms would provide the conceptual basis for the Christians, which merged the Liverpool soul tradition with post-punk attitude and a distinctly socially conscious edge. As the group's manager, Pete Fulwell, explains:

> I encouraged a group of people to come together as the Christians. We did a deal with Island Records and the album just went boom. The idea was inspired really by Two-Tone and I loved that, I loved the whole attitude of Jerry Dammers [of the Specials and co-founder of Two-Tone Records] and all that stuff, I loved it. It was all based on ska and I remember at the time thinking, if you could do this with soul … it would work [with] R&B…. But nobody did, and then I heard these guys the Christian Brothers singing something on TV, just [a] cover version and [I] thought, there it is. Put that together with somebody who is coming from a new-wave background and something interesting would happen. That first album did do very well. It was … the biggest-selling debut album ever on Island Records. We sold about 1.5 million of that album just in the UK.

Conclusion

The eventual success of both the Real Thing and the Christians perhaps signifies the fruition of a local musical tradition linked to the particular history of migration and settlement in Liverpool, a story which has been under-represented in histories of music in the city. These individual histories illustrate a complex set of global/local relationships in terms of the black diaspora and culture in two main ways. First, they illuminate how the specific socio-cultural contexts of Liverpool resulted in an environment in which African-American music became highly meaningful within the social practices of the L8 area and beyond. Secondly, they are indicative of how diasporic musical practices are often characterized by the inscription of locality into globalized musical forms. In other words, in the hands of Liverpool artists, doo-wop, soul and disco became re-articulated to engage with and reflect the specificities of the Liverpool black experience. We can further understand this inscription of locality as part of a web of exchange and dialogue across the diaspora, which flows in a variety of directions. As Gilroy (1997: 341) notes, a 'new structure of cultural exchange has been built up across the imperial networks which once played host to the triangular trade of sugar, slaves and capital', carrying 'ideas, ideologies, theologies and philosophies'. The Real Thing's 'Children of the Ghetto' is a case in point here. What was written as an expression of Liverpool black identity has been adapted to address social issues across the diaspora through cover versions by a wide range of artists, including Philip Bailey (of Earth, Wind and Fire), Mary J. Blige (one of the biggest names in US R&B), the UK jazz pioneer Courtney Pine, Paul Hardcastle, the French R&B band Native and the Canadian rapper Capeech.

The oral histories presented here also reveal dimensions that are often ignored within histories of the UK recording industry and within the wider historicization of UK black music. The experiences of black Liverpool musicians hint at an undercurrent of prejudice within the media and a lack of institutional support that served to stall their careers. This is clearly an area of the UK music industry and media history that is ripe for further research, and a wider survey of British black musicians and industry personnel is long overdue. In actuality, there is a paucity of historical work on British black music more generally and especially in relation to soul music. What work that does exist in this area (Chambers 1985; Wood 2001; BBC 2007) tends to rely upon a reductive historical narrative encompassing London-based acts of the 1970s and northern soul. It has been the aim of this chapter to make an initial contribution in redressing this imbalance, but there is much more work to be done. Only by uncovering these hidden histories and representing the experiences of these musical pioneers can we fully address the significance and contribution that they have made to the UK's musical history.

Notes

1   Christian (2000), for instance, points to the problematic nature of defining a singular 'black community', as a variety of identities can exist simultaneously, such as 'black, black British, Liverpool-born black, Scouse black' and so on.

2 See, for instance, the discussion by Cohen (2007: 196–97), and the 1995 Granada Television documentary *Who Put the Beat in Merseybeat?*

3 The *Empire Windrush* was a merchant vessel which docked at Tilbury on 22 June 1948 carrying around 500 Caribbean passengers (possibly many more – see Mead 2009). The *Windrush* has become an important symbol within British culture, often being 'understood as metonymic of the postwar boom in immigration into Britain' (Mead 2009: 137).

4 It should be noted that Liverpool has a history of producing prominent black musicians since the nineteenth century. The famous Jazz musician Gordon Stretton, for instance, was born (1887) and started his career in the city.

5 RAF Burtonwood was an airbase near Warrington, around fifteen miles from Liverpool. It operated as the supply and maintenance base for the US Airforce in Europe from the US entry into the Second World War until the 1970s.

6 It is interesting that Lynch is another figure who tends to be entirely absent from histories of black British music.

7 A US hit for the Drifters.

8 Eddie Amoo quoted at www.alwynwturner.com/glitter/real_thing.html (accessed April 2009).

9 Steve Higginson, at www.geocities.com/soulpool (accessed April 2009).

10 Fryer (1997), for instance, notes that 'the format of *Top of the Pops* [the most popular UK television pop show] originally favoured white, British styles' and that even in the 1970s 'Soul, disco, and reggae appearances were restricted, unlike white rock, to chart entries. Even then, coverage was seldom as good or as extensive. Many disco records were only played over the credits, or with a dance troupe performing.'

References

Back, Les (1996) *New Ethnicities and Urban Culture: Racisms and Multiculture in Young Lives*. London: Routledge.

BBC (2007) *Soul Britannia*. Television documentary.

Bolland, Philip (2010) 'Sonic Geography, Place and Race in the Formation of Local Identity: Liverpool and Scousers'. *Geografiska Annaler: Series B, Human Geography* 92(1): 1–22.

Brocken, Michael (2010) *Other Voices: Hidden Histories of Liverpool's Popular Music Scenes, 1930s–1970s*. Aldershot: Ashgate.

Chambers, Ian (1985) *Urban Rhythms: Pop Music and Popular Culture*. New York: St Martin's Press.

Christian, Mark (1998) 'An African-Centered Approach to the Black British Experience: With Special Reference to Liverpool'. *Journal of Black Studies* 28(3): 291–308.

Christian, Mark (2000) *Multiracial Identity: An International Perspective*. London: Macmillan.

Christian, Mark (2002) *Black Identity in the Twentieth Century: Expressions of the US and UK African Diaspora*. London: Hansib.

Clayson, Alan (1997) *Hamburg: The Cradle of British Rock*. London: Sanctuary.

Cohen, Sara (2007) *Decline, Renewal and the City in Popular Music Culture: Beyond the Beatles*. Aldershot: Ashgate.

Cohen, Sara and Kevin McManus (1991) *Harmonious Relations: Popular Music* in *Family Life on Merseyside*. Liverpool: National Museums and Galleries on Merseyside.

Du Noyer, Paul (2002) *Liverpool: Wondrous Place – Music from the Cavern to Cream*. London: Virgin.

Fryer, Paul (1997) '"Everybody's on Top of the Pops": Popular Music on British Television 1960–1985'. *Popular Music and Society* 2(2): 71–89.

Gilroy, Paul (1996) *The Black Atlantic: Modernity and Double Consciousness*. London: Verso.

Gilroy, Paul (1997) 'Diaspora, Utopia and the Critique of Capitalism'. In: Ken Gelder and Sarah Thornton (eds) *The Subcultures Reader*. New York: Routledge. pp. 340–49.

Hebdige, Dick (1987) *Cut'n'Mix: Culture, Identity and Caribbean Music*. London: Comedia/Methuen.

Hesmondhalgh, David and Caspar Melville (2001) 'Urban Breakbeat Culture: Repercussions of Hiphop in the UK'. In: Tony Mitchell (ed.) *Global Noise: Rap and Hiphop Outside the US*. Middletown, CT: Wesleyan University Press. pp. 86–110.

Hiro, Dilip (1971) *Black British, White British*. London: Monthly Review Press.

Martelli, Rita (2006) Unpublished essay 'Black Music in Liverpool'. Institute of Popular Music, University of Liverpool.

McGrath, James (2010) 'A Little Help From Their Friends'. *Big Issue in the North*, 29 March. pp. 18–19.

Mead, Matthew (2009) '*Empire Windrush*: The Cultural Memory of an Imaginary Arrival'. *Journal of Postcolonial Writing* 45(2): 137–49.

Nassy Brown, Jaqueline (1998) 'Black Liverpool, Black America, and the Gendering of Diasporic Space'. *Cultural Anthropology* 13(3): 291–325.

Nassy Brown, Jaqueline (2006) 'Gendering "Black America" in Black Liverpool'. In: Kamari Maxine Clarke and Deborah A. Thomas (eds) *Globalization and Race Transformations in the Cultural Production of Blackness*. Durham, NC: Duke University Press. pp. 73–92.

Oliver, Paul (1990) *Black Music in Britain: Essays on the Afro-Asian Contribution to Popular Music*. Milton Keynes: Open University Press.

Small, Stephen (2002) 'Black People of Mixed Origins and the Politics of Identity'. In: Mark Christian (ed.) *Black Identity in the 20th Century: Expressions of the US and UK African Diaspora*. London: Hansib. pp. 167–94.

Webb, Peter (2007) *Exploring the Networked Worlds of Popular Music*. London: Routledge.

Wilson, Greg (2004) 'Les Spaine', at www.electrofunkroots.co.uk/interviews/les_spaine.html (accessed April 2009).

Wood, Andy (2001) 'Soul'. In: Alison Donnell (ed.) *Companion to Contemporary Black British Culture*. London: Routledge. pp. 285–86.

Oral histories

Eddie Amoo, National Museums Liverpool, 29 April 2008.

Joe Ankrah, National Museums Liverpool, 4 June 2008.

Garry Christian, National Museums Liverpool, 4 June 2008.

Chief Angus Chukuemeka, National Museums Liverpool, 26 August 2008.

Sugar Deen, National Museums Liverpool, 4 June 2008.

George Dixon, National Museums Liverpool, 29 July 2008.

Pete Fulwell, National Museums Liverpool, 14 May 2008.

CHAPTER 6

Not just one of the boys: gender, representation and the historical record

Marion Leonard

Introduction

In 2006 research got underway for *The Beat Goes On*, an exhibition exploring popular music on Merseyside which would open at World Museum Liverpool as part of the celebrations for the year of Liverpool being the European Capital of Culture (2008). As research progressed it became apparent that the histories and contributions of local female musicians were not as visible or as well documented as those of their male contemporaries. This chapter takes this fact as its starting point, and investigates both how gender might have an effect upon decisions to become a musician and the experience of being a female musician in a male-dominated industry. The aim of the chapter is to address a series of questions provoked by the observation that women's participation within the local music scene was something of a hidden history: Why are women not more visible on the local scene and in histories of Liverpool music? In what ways are the histories of local female performers documented and how might this be informed by attitudes to gender? How do local female performers discuss the ways in which attitudes to gender might have influenced their careers or the ways in which they experienced the music industry in the course of their careers? The chapter argues that it is important to take account of the histories of female musicians not just to offer a more representative historical record but to examine how music practice and the sources which document this practice are informed by attitudes to gender.

Gender and participation

Part of the reason why men tend to dominate the history of Liverpool music is that women have generally not been as publicly present as music makers, and so written accounts and archive holdings reflect a gender imbalance in terms of participation. In this respect Liverpool reflects a national trend, as British music scenes, from jazz to rock, have tended to be male dominated. This gender imbalance can be seen in the ratio of female musicians performing in bands and as solo artists through to the presence of women in other areas of the music industry, such as studio production and management. For example, a 1989 survey of 289 people working in the Liverpool music industry found that 'only thirteen of them were women, six of whom worked in music journalism' (Cohen 1997: 19). In research focused on the indie music scene in the city, Cohen (1997: 18) noted that the 'vast majority of musicians are men and most of the several hundred or so bands are all-male. Of the minority of women musicians involved, most are singers and there are perhaps one or two all-women bands.' The absence of female artists has been so marked that in 2004 the BBC Liverpool website ran an appeal requesting that female musicians 'get in touch so we can redress the balance'.[1] The situation is reflective of a more general gender bias within the music industry at a regional, national and international level. Focusing on the north-west region of the UK, a music industry report noted that 'there are barriers to growth, for music entrepreneurs and creative individuals in terms of gender' (Burns Owens Partnership 2006: 120). While there is no research into the proportion of musicians in the north-west who are female, statistics published by Creative and Cultural Skills (2008) detail that 63 per cent of people working in the music industry in the region, across all sectors, are male.

This in turn raises other questions, not least of which is why the participation of women is lower than that of men. Answering this is complicated, as consideration has to be given to a variety of social and cultural factors which can affect the number of women becoming and sustaining careers as musicians (the focus of this chapter) or working within the industry more widely. Many of these factors will not be especially local in nature, although they will be experienced at a local level. Attitudes related to gender can directly create barriers to entry or, more subtly perhaps, sustain masculine cultures within professional music environments which are discouraging to women. Numerous scholars have attended to the issue of how gender impacts upon music practice. For example, Lucy Green (1997) has examined how gender stereotypes are operational from a very early age and can affect the development of music skills. Green's research found that school teachers and pupils perpetuate ideas about gender which result in girls being less likely to opt for popular music performance, while boys feel encouraged to engage with noisy, assertive playing styles. Other studies have highlighted the different ways in which popular music has become associated with masculinity, from the macho posturing of heavy metal (Walser 1993) through to the gendering of rock instrumentation (Bayton 1997; Clawson 1999) and the way in which music technology has been targeted at male audiences (Théberge 1991; Keightley 1996). Attitudes about gender can, then, be powerful in encouraging certain behaviours, attitudes and modes of participation in music practice which can work to exclude female participation.

Female music makers

In addition to these wider gendered patterns of socialization there are also broader issues relating to representation which have an active effect upon the visibility of women within the history of popular music. Written histories and music press accounts of popular music tend to be grounded within particular critical conventions, which follow set ways of ascribing historical importance and often fail to account for certain types of participation. This can partly explain for the relative invisibility of female performers within written accounts of Liverpool's music history, despite the long history of female music makers who have emerged from the city. Indeed, Liverpool's first number one artist was a woman: Lita Roza's 1953 hit with the novelty song '(How Much Is) That Doggie in the Window?' also brought her the accolade of becoming the first British woman to top the newly established singles chart. Cilla Black followed up this commercial success with a string of chart hits throughout the 1960s. Subsequent female pop performers from Merseyside have also made an impact on the charts, from Sonia and the Reynolds Girls (both produced by Stock, Aitken and Waterman) to the highly successful 2000s pop of Atomic Kitten, the Sugababes and Melanie Chisholm. Despite their high level of visibility in their respective eras, these women's contributions tend to be ignored or underplayed within historical accounts. This is perhaps due to implicit notions of value embedded within popular music historiography, whereby certain genres or types of artist are considered more important than others. These unashamedly mainstream musicians do not fit with the dominant historicization, which places rock above other forms within a hierarchy of musical value. Roza, for instance, is often rather dismissively remembered for her novelty hit, despite the fact that she was the lead singer with the Ted Heath Orchestra, one of the most important and most popular big bands of the era, and was voted 'Top British Female Singer' in the *New Musical Express* (*NME*) in five consecutive years, 1951–55. Similarly, in retrospect, Cilla Black's powerful interpretation of some of the finest pop songwriting of the 1960s tends to be overshadowed by her subsequent television career, which has led to her being critically neglected in comparison with her contemporaries Dusty Springfield and Petula Clarke.

Other women involved within a variety of local scenes across a range of genres have also tended to be relatively undocumented, albeit for differing reasons. For example, although characterized as a male scene, there were numerous vocal groups such as the Mystics, the Three Bells, the Charmers and the Blue Notes active within the Merseybeat circuit, as well as a number of female-fronted bands, such as the Flintstones, Tiffany's Dimension, and Jeanie and the Big Guys (who recorded for PYE).[2] There were also all-female beat groups such as the Demoiselles and most prominently the Liver Birds, who, forming in 1962, were one of the first all-female R&B groups in the world, and who scored several chart hits and television appearances in Germany (see Brocken 2010: 150–53). Another artist who emerged at this time was Beryl Marsden, who made a number of solo records and contributed powerful R&B vocals to acts such as Shotgun Express, and Johnny B and the Quotations. Female during the 1950s was rather mannered and dry. It was not until the 1960s, with the development of so-called 'new journalism', that music writing took on a more stylistic flair, designed to communicate the atmosphere and emotion of a performance while also bringing the personality of the journalist into the account. While the factual style of reporting of the earlier period, with its linear descriptions of live performances, may now seem rather outmoded, the details are very useful in tracing through the professional engagements and fortunes of performers. In addition to detailing Roza's stage costumes, these accounts also show her business decision making as she developed her career. The *NME* of 9 April 1954 (p. 7), for example, noted that she was unhappy with her record label, Decca, and had requested to be released from her contract, stating a preference for Philips. The reports also document her decision to leave the Ted Heath Orchestra and become 'the first post-war British band girl singer to go into variety as a solo star at the top of the bill' (Kinn 1954). Kinn notes that this savvy decision would afford her a much better income. Press accounts are thus a useful documentary source for tracing performer histories. They provide an insight into the business decisions and career stages of Lita Roza as well as the gendered attitudes which were prevalent in the business at the time.

One might expect that contemporary journalism would steer away from overtly sexist descriptions and the sidelining of female stars. However, an examination of the coverage of female artists in the press in recent years still reveals bias in terms of gender. The media descriptions of Abi Harding, saxophonist and backing vocalist with the Zutons, can be taken as an example. Press coverage in the UK's regional and national press often described Harding in terms of her appearance rather than commenting on her musical contribution. She has been described as 'glamorous' (Mansey 2006; Wright 2008), 'hugely photogenic, perfectly-legged' (Quirk 2006), a 'sax bomb' (*Liverpool Daily Echo*, 23 August 2007: 18), who adds 'leggy glamour' (Aizlewood 2006) and a 'sexy bird with great legs' (*Daily Mirror*, 8 August 2008: 7). Similarly the picture captions to photographs of Harding published in the press have been given titles such as 'sax appeal' (*Daily Mirror*, 8 August 2008: 7), 'saxy and sexy' (Thompson 2008) and 'sax siren' (Traynor 2007). With some parallels to Roza's press coverage, journalists also comment on her choice of stage clothes, for example drawing attention to her 'tiny black dress that showed off those fabulous legs' (Wright 2008), her 'slinky black dress and thigh high boots [which] grabbed much of the attention on stage' (Dayani 2008) and her 'gold Miu Miu "puffball" dress [which] matched her gold saxophone' (Alexander 2006b). In addition to these descriptions, journalists very frequently included the detail that Harding and fellow band member Sean Payne are partners. Significantly, Harding is described as Payne's girlfriend (Duerden 2006; Heawood 2008; *Liverpool Daily Echo*, 15 January 2009: 4), partner (Flockhart 2008; Martin 2008) or fiancée (Wright 2007), while Payne is never referred to as Harding's boyfriend. This has the effect that Harding is presented as a possession of Sean rather than a band member in her own right; indeed, the frequency with which this partnership is mentioned to some extent calls into question her position as an equal in the band. The representation of Harding within these press accounts can thus be critiqued as limited, reductive and often dismissive.

Oral histories

While press reports clearly offer a valuable source of detail about performers and the critical reception of their work, the above examples demonstrate that they also frequently frame female performers in particular and problematic ways. One way of addressing the absences and biases within journalistic and other historical accounts is to seek out alternative narratives to enhance our understanding of music histories. Oral histories are very valuable in this regard, as they can often work to disrupt or question dominant narratives and ways of constructing history. As Alexander (2006a: 10) argues, oral histories can be particularly valuable in providing details and per-spectives which are missing from archive collections, making them 'ideally suited to the recovery of the historical absences that scar all archives'. Indeed, interviews and oral histories have been a key way through which various writers have sought to document female par-ticipation in music cultures in an attempt to correct histories which have ignored or marginalized women's contribution (Evans 1994, Gourse 1995; Juno 1996; Post 1997). In researching *The Beat Goes On* exhibition, oral histories were important not only as a way to fill gaps in existing accounts but also to enable the inclusion of details

Lita Roza, the first British woman and first Liverpool artist to reach number one.

Bill Harry, founder of the bi-weekly publication *Mersey Beat*, which did much to popularize the term 'Merseybeat'.

The Chants at the Cavern Club. The Beatles played as the backing band when the Chants made their first appearance at the Cavern in November 1962.

The Beatles appearing on *The Ed Sullivan Show* in 1964, which was watched by more than 73 million viewers. It is widely regarded as one of the defining moments in twentieth-century popular culture.

Gerry Marsden and Cilla Black, two of the most popular Merseybeat artists of the 1960s.

Beryl Marsden with Lee Curtis' All-Stars, one of the multitude of Liverpool acts to play regularly in Hamburg.

Supercharge at the Sportsman pub, St Johns precinct, where the band attracted a huge local following in the early 1970s.

Exterior of St Johns precinct, with the Top Rank Suite ballroom in view. The precinct was a centre for music performance and entertainment in the early 1970s.

The Real Thing, who topped the charts in the 1970s; their *Four From Eight* album became one of the definitive statements of British soul music.

Eric's flyer, designed by Steve Hardstaff, who has also produced artwork for releases by numerous Merseyside bands, including Brenda and the Beach Balls, Half Man Half Biscuit and the Icicle Works.

Club regular Mark Jordan and friends outside Eric's on Mathew Street in the late 1970s. The street became a centre for Liverpool's creative life during this period.

From creative hub to tourist destination: the Mathew Street festival has become one of the largest free music festivals in Europe.

Big in Japan, featuring Holly Johnson, Jayne Casey and Bill Drummond.

Deaf School performing at Eric's. Emerging from the city's art school, the band was central to the scene which produced a number of highly successful acts of the 1980s.

Ian McCulloch playing with Echo and the Bunnymen at Caird Hall, Dundee, in the early 1980s.

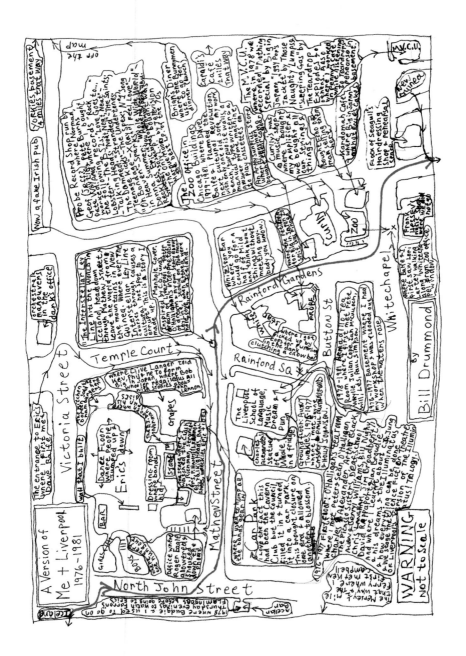

Bill Drummond's hand-drawn map of central Liverpool in the late 1970s.

John Power performing with Cast at the Earthbeat festival, Sefton Park, Liverpool.

Mick and John Head of the much-loved Liverpool band Shack.

Woman with Cream logo tattoo at Amnesia, Ibiza. Cream inspired an intense devotion among clubbers and went from the back room of the Academy club to a global brand in the space of a decade.

Quadrant Park, Bootle. The former snooker hall became one of the first legal all-night clubs of the acid-house era in the UK and made a significant impact on Liverpool's dance music scene.

Garry Christian, solo artist and lead singer of the Christians. The band mixed Liverpool's soul tradition with post-punk attitude, and gained international success during the 1980s.

Ian McNabb. From his days with the Icicle Works through to his solo work, his songwriting has frequently reflected Liverpool's social and cultural life.

Liverpool-born singer, guitarist and songwriter Kathryn Williams.

The Coral's James Skelly recording the *Roots and Echoes* album at Wheeler End studio, summer 2006.

Abi Harding of the Zutons performing at Knowsley festival in 2007.

One of the boys?

The fact that female musicians are often distinguished as different from the 'norm' can help to explain why some are reluctant to discuss issues of gender in interviews. They may not wish to position themselves as remarkable or different because they are women working in a male-dominated field. The comments of two Liverpool performers working in very different music styles and contexts can help to illustrate this point. Lita Roza discussed her experience of touring as a singer with the Ted Heath Orchestra during the early 1950s. The schedule was very demanding and Roza commented that they would be expected to perform every night:

> We'd probably do a one-night stand in Nottingham and come back by coach and be at Aeolian Hall [in London] for a broadcast at nine o'clock the following morning. It was hard, it was hard singing with the band because you're doing one-nighters travelling up and down the country ... you could do seven different cities in the week.

When asked if she found it challenging to be the only woman performing with the band, she replied, 'Well they always thought of me as one of the boys because, you know, I wasn't, you know, you've got to be one of the boys with a band of fifteen musicians'. Her comments reveal a pragmatism concerning the need to fit in and get along with fellow musicians. The phrase being 'one of the boys' suggests that she was accepted into the camaraderie of the touring ensemble. Blues vocalist Connie Lush echoed these comments when she was questioned about her experience of working within a male-dominated environment. She commented, 'It may not be what women want me to say but, working with guys all the time, I think I have become one of the guys in a strange way'. This rhetorical move is noteworthy for both musicians, as it demonstrates a desire and assertion by them that they should not be singled out as atypical because of their sex. Lush's remark contends that she is so much part of a fraternity of musicians that she has *become* 'one of the guys'. This is not to say that Lush was unwilling to discuss her experience of negotiating the expectations of gender within her working life as a musician. She commented:

> I used to have a really big view on it at one time and it was very negative. But really I think, as I have grown with the music and

everything, I just want to be thought of as a musician. It is not an easy
world to be in. It is not an easy world for the guys. I mean, they have
to think about image the same – although their shelf life is longer but,
hey, that's the way it goes. But you have to be tough, extra tough I
think as a woman to be in the business. Even more so now because it
is so image and money conscious.

Her comments acknowledge that gender does have an impact on
her practice but also stress the importance of being understood as a
musician first, rather than being marginalized as a female musician.

The comments by these musicians that they were effectively
'one of the boys' is indicative of imperatives around masculinity
and femininity which are at work within certain environments at
particular times. These oral histories explain how musicians work
within and experience music practice as gendered subjects. In part,
then, these histories open up new avenues for investigation and
offer a different way of telling histories which might challenge or
at least nuance existing accounts. Oral histories of male performers
can similarly be understood as offering gendered accounts, often
including details of male companionship and tales of on-the-road
antics, which construct masculinity in particular ways. However, the
accounts of male musicians have not tended to be read in terms of
gender but have been held up as examples of rock-and-roll excess, as
tales of expected or predictably anarchic behaviour. What has gone
unsaid here is that this masculine behaviour is expected of musicians
because musicians are also 'expected' to be male. The oral histories of
female musicians throw these assumptions into relief and allow us to
critique some of the practices of music culture in new ways.

Gender and the experience of musical cultures

Oral history work with female musicians is important not only in
writing women back into historical accounts from which they are
missing but also in offering alternative perspectives on dominant
narratives of history. Jayne Casey's recollections of the music scene
surrounding Liverpool's Eric's club serve as an example of this.
Casey was lead singer in the punk band Big in Japan in the 1970s.
The band had a changing line-up which at points included Ian
Broudie (who went on to found the Lightning Seeds), Holly Johnson

(who later became the lead singer of Frankie Goes To Hollywood), Bill Drummond (who established KLF) and Budgie, drummer in Siouxsie and the Banshees. Casey reflects that her experience of the music scene was different to that of many of her contemporaries, as she was a female musician participating in a male-dominated scene: 'if I sit down with the lads and talk about it sometimes it is like we were on different universes, never mind different clubs. It was a totally different experience, experiencing it as a woman.' Casey reflected that gender had an impact in many ways, from her negotiation of expected roles of femininity through to the female artists who inspired her. Her style choices, such as the decision at one point to shave her head, also signalled a refutation of traditional gender roles and modes of feminine display. As she explains: 'It was an attempt to get away from what was considered female sexuality. I was a very, very unusual-looking young woman.' Casey comments that it is important not just to consider the male dominance of the Eric's scene but to take account of the longer history and characterization of rock and roll, which has become defined as a male practice: 'The image of rock and roll is a male image so genderwise you were a girl amongst a load of lads. And trying to hold your own amongst a load of lads.' She went on:

> I had a little bit of a problem with the stereotypical rock-and-roll image because you could feel as a singer it was hindering you. It is such a powerful image: four boys in leather jackets on a stage. You know, it has been with us for years. So it was something that you had to consider all the time and you knew lads made friends easier with the music journalists and things.

Casey's remarks point to the ways in which the male dominance and masculine iconography of rock music, alongside particular social practices, can work to marginalize women participants.

Similarly, Beryl Marsden commented on how masculine and feminine roles were clearly defined when she was performing in the 1960s and as such could dictate work opportunities. She recalls that her role as singer with the Undertakers was curtailed because her youthful schoolgirl image was not deemed suitable for the rock-and-roll direction of the band:

> The Undertakers went off to Germany to the Star Club in Hamburg. And when they came back they were all sort of grown up and wearing

all black gear and didn't want a young little female singer with them spoiling their image. I actually sang a bit for a little while with Freddie Starr and Derry Wilkie and with Faron. I sort of sang with everyone at the time. Not actually on the road but just in the clubs a little bit because I was waiting for the Undertakers to come back. So when that kind of happened and they were going off doing their macho stuff then I joined Lee Curtis.[5]

In this case expectations around gender actually shaped the direction of Marsden's career, closing down and opening up particular opportunities. Her reflections illustrate how oral testimony can reveal aspects of popular music practice which written histories, with their conventions and discrete historicizing traits, do not.

Conclusion

Attending to issues of gender and female representation within Liverpool's popular music history is, then, not just about adjusting the history books or campaigning for new names to be added to the canon. It is valuable in understanding how constructions of masculinity and femininity are at work within music scenes and how participation and historicization are informed by gendered attitudes. As Mary Ann Villarreal found when undertaking oral history work with Mexican-American women in the music industry, the material she collected was richer and gave her a much deeper insight into social history than she had anticipated. The experiences of these women offered details of working life, audiences, entertainment spaces and music careers which did not appear in secondary literature or most press accounts and thus 'produced a picture yet to be painted' (Villarreal 2006: 64). Similarly, the accounts given within this chapter work to paint in new details on existing narratives and offer different perspectives on musical practices. While the chapter has examined only a handful of cases, it nevertheless reveals patterns that add to our understanding of how different musical worlds operate in relation to gender. By focusing on music makers from one particular city, it is also possible to unpack how gender is navigated in different circumstances and through local cultures. Clearly, the music and media industries have not been gender blind and so it is important that, in appraising local music history, we are

Tucker, Sherrie (1999) 'Telling Performances: Jazz History Remembered and Remade by the Women in the Band'. *Oral History Review* 26(1): 67–84.

Villarreal, Mary Ann (2006) 'Finding Our Place: Reconstructing Community Through Oral History'. *Oral History Review* 33(2): 45–64.

Walser, Robert (1993) *Running With the Devil: Power, Gender, and Madness in Heavy Metal Music*. Hanover, NH: Wesleyan University Press.

Wright, Jade (2007) 'Music: Amy and MTV: What a FAB Year'. *Liverpool Daily Echo*, 28 December. p. 3 (first edition).

Wright, Jade (2008) 'The Zutons, Echo Arena: Review'. *Liverpool Daily Echo*, 22 December. p. 19.

Oral histories

Jayne Casey, National Museums Liverpool, 27 February 2009.

Connie Lush, National Museums Liverpool, 25 June 2008.

Lita Roza, National Museums Liverpool, 15 May 2007.

Kathryn Williams, National Museums Liverpool, 13 June 2008.

CHAPTER 7

Liverpool's 1970s bohemia: Deaf School, Eric's and the post-punk scene

Robert Strachan

Introduction

Eric's club opened in October 1976 on Mathew Street, opposite the site of the original Cavern, as a joint venture between Roger Eagle (a DJ and promoter), Ken Testi (road manager for the band Deaf School) and Pete Fulwell (a graphic designer). It would go on to be the most significant Liverpool club of the punk and post-punk eras, until it closed, under a hail of protest, in March 1980. Despite its relatively short lifespan, Eric's has assumed legendary status in Liverpool's musical community. The importance of the club within Liverpool music culture's sense of itself is perhaps unsurprising, given that many of the central figures within the Eric's scene went on to enjoy an unprecedented level of critical and commercial success. Orchestral Manoeuvres in the Dark (OMD), Echo and the Bunnymen, Dead or Alive, the Teardrop Explodes, the Lightning Seeds, Simply Red, It's Immaterial, the Christians, Frankie Goes to Hollywood and the KLF either started at Eric's or included members who spent a formative stage of their careers at the club.

Eric's can be understood as a focal point of a particular and inter-disciplinary creative scene. In mapping out the broader picture of this scene it is important also to plot a number of other venues and institutions. These include the Liverpool Stadium (a boxing venue on Moorfields, in the financial district), where Roger Eagle had been instrumental in promoting 'underground' music acts before the establishment of Eric's. Eagle had previously been the DJ at the Twisted Wheel in Manchester, which was one of the first clubs in the UK to play what became known as northern soul. Geoff Davies' Liverpool record shop, Probe Records, was also important as a hang-out space for scene members and as somewhere to discover new music, recommended by this influential city 'taste maker' (Brocken 2010: 213). Probe Records was first established in 1970 on Clarence Street, near to the city universities; by 1974 Davies had added another branch, in the boutique of Silly Billy's in White-chapel, before going on to found the fondly remembered store in Button Street, just off Mathew Street. The Liverpool Art School, in the Hope Street area, was the nexus of a vibrant creative scene in the mid-1970s. Deaf School, a band formed by students and lecturers at the school, were mixing performance art, poetry and theatre with an eclectic approach to rock music. The nine-member band attracted a strong local following before going on to make three albums for Warner Brothers, leaving a lasting legacy on the Liverpool post-punk scene. The Art School was also the home of another performance-art-inspired group, known variously as Albert Dock, Albert Dock and the Cod Warriors and Albert Dock and the Codfish Warriors, before it mutated into the power-pop group the Yachts.

While many of these distinct elements of Liverpool's bohemian life had existed throughout the 1970s, by 1976 many had converged upon the Mathew Street area. As well as providing a new home for Probe Records, it was also the location of the Liverpool School of Language, Music, Dream and Pun, a creative space opened in an old warehouse building. Local entrepreneur Peter O'Halligan bought the warehouse in 1974 and created a quasi-mystical mythology about the building, claiming it to be on the exact spot that Carl Jung identified in a 1927 dream about the location of the 'pool of life' (see Jones and Wilks-Heeg 2007: 209–12). The building housed several significant Liverpool underground institutions. O'Halligan's tea rooms on the first floor doubled up as a gallery cum theatre which would host events such as the Even Moore exhibition (consisting of paintings rejected by the prestigious John Moores Contemporary Painting competition) and, significantly, Ken Campbell's *Illuminatus!* plays (under the guise of Liverpool Science Fiction Theatre) in late 1976 (see Florek 2007: 173). In 1975 ex-hairdresser Jayne Casey set up Aunt Twackies, a vintage clothes store on the ground floor (where Paul Rutherford, later of Liverpool's first punk band the Spitfire Boys and the internationally successful pop act Frankie Goes to Hollywood, also worked), while the basement provided studio space for artists including Bill Drummond (later of Big in Japan and the KLF). In the short time after the opening of Eric's this creative clustering would become even more concentrated. The Armadillo Tea Rooms would provide another key meeting place for artists and musicians, and the area would house office space for OMD and Zoo Records, the label set up by Drummond and Dave Balfe which would release the early singles by Echo and the Bunnymen and Teardrop Explodes.

This chapter uses the oral histories of some key players to trace these emergent strands and situate the legacy of Eric's within a wider context – a bohemian thread in the city's culture where art, design, theatre, fashion and music intersected. Fittingly, the oral histories drawn upon here are from musicians who came from this interdisciplinary background. Steve Allen, for example, came from an art school background and went on to sing (as Enrico Cadillac) for Deaf School. Two other graduates of the Liverpool School of Art, Martin Dempsey and Bill Drummond, also offer their recollections. Dempsey played in a variety of influential Liverpool groups, from the new wave of the Yachts in the late 1970s to the sophisticated chart pop of It's Immaterial and the cult proto-grunge of the Melotones in the 1980s. Drummond went on to be a founder member of the Liverpool group Big in Japan and would later score several international hits with KLF and the Timelords, which would eventually mutate into the situationist style art organization the K Foundation. Big in Japan was also the first major musical project of Jayne Casey and Ian Broudie. After that group disbanded Casey formed Pink Military and Pink Industry and has been a visible figure in Liverpool's creative landscape ever since, being centrally involved in Cream and the European Capital of Culture programme 2008. Ian Broudie would go on to play in the Original Mirrors and the Lightning Seeds, a chart-topping band of the 1990s, as well as being a successful producer for bands including Icicle Works, Echo and the Bunneymen, the Coral and the Zutons. Aside from these musicians, the chapter also draws upon the oral histories of other participants within the Eric's scene. Hilary Steele offers comments as an Eric's regular who was inspired by the vibrancy of the scene to become an unofficial photographer of the club throughout its existence (many of her photographs can be found in Florek and Whelan 2009). After starting off as a graphic designer, Pete Fulwell was one of the founders of Eric's who also founded Zoo records and managed the Christians, perhaps the most successful UK soul group of the 1980s. Norman Killon started his DJing career at the Sink Club, Liverpool's foremost R&B club, before working behind the counter in Probe Records and DJing at Eric's.

The chapter is intended as a window onto the way in which creativity is socially produced and offers an important example of how social and geographical factors can lead to new creative trajectories. The recollections demonstrate how music and information about music are shared and prioritized by key taste makers, and are fed into a wider shared aesthetic within a particular social network. For example, several respondents point to the way in which Roger Eagle and Probe Records' staff served to broaden people's musical horizons and transmit ideas relating to musical value within the scene. The chapter provides a thick description of an environment where ideas became cross-fertilized across artistic forms. In a discussion of a concurrent post-punk scene centred around New York's Mudd Club and Artists Space, Gendron (2002) points to a 'borderline aesthetic' whereby social cross-overs between avant-garde and popular music communities result in hybridized artistic forms such as punk-art and no-wave. A similar 'art/pop engagement' (Gendron 2002) can be found in the narrative constructed here and it is worth noting that similar art-scene/working-class coalitions were characteristic of other punk and post-punk scenes in the UK, in cities such as London and Leeds (see Savage 1991; Reynolds 2005).

However, the oral histories included in this chapter demonstrate that, perhaps logically, the art and music cross-over that occurred in Liverpool took on specifically local inflections. We can trace lines, for instance, between the quasi-mysticism of Peter O'Halligan's vision of Mathew Street and the work of Julian Cope; between Geoff Davies' evangelism for West Coast psychedelia and the psychedelic tendencies of Echo and the Bunnymen and the Teardrop Explodes; between the art school bricolage of Deaf School and Big in Japan and Frankie Goes to Hollywood; between Ken Campbell's

Liverpool Science Fiction Theatre and the constructed mythology of Bill Drummond's later work with the KLF. These tangential connections highlight the importance of the specificity of place to the creativity of the individuals within a particular creative scene, and are indicative here of the distinct musical and artistic characteristics of creativity within the city. As Grunenberg and Knifton (2007: 28) note, Liverpool 'seems to foster its own sense of the avant-garde: a democratic grass-roots culture that negotiates art, everyday life, mass culture and politics'.

Thus, while the life and legacy of Eric's have been covered admirably elsewhere (Du Noyer 2002; Florek 2007; Florek and Whelan 2009) and the club has been seen as so significant that it has even had a stage musical written about it, this chapter contributes to this material with previously unpublished oral histories, which are woven together with some key accounts from other people on this scene in order to tell the story of this creative milieu through the words of those who were part of it. The aim is to give a broader picture of the creative scene within the city of which Eric's was a part. The different contributors are deliberately left to speak for themselves, sometimes giving conflicting accounts of events and offering differing opinions. Like creativity itself, oral history and memory defy neat delineated edges, in that they are subject to highly personal interpretations and give a subjective prioritization of what the individual finds meaningful. In any case, it is not the intention of this chapter to scrutinize the veracity of individual reflections or to construct a simple historical narrative. Rather, it aims to offer individual perspectives on how musicians and scene members experienced this particular moment in Liverpool's cultural history and how they articulate its continued importance as a seminal moment in the city's creative life. Thus, the narrators of this chapter have a tendency to couch their descriptions of historical events in terms of how it was experienced by them as individuals and how events were crucial in establishing the community to which they belonged. As Allen (1984: 7) has noted, this has been a key way in which narrators of oral histories can uncover important revelations about a particular community and in 'using these structural units of historical experience as the basis for talking about the past, members reveal from their own perspective what the community and its history are all about'.

Mathew Street in the 1970s

BILL DRUMMOND: I came to art school in Liverpool because John Lennon had been to our art school. I mean it was that corny and although I've gone on record saying that I think *Sgt. Peppers* is the worst thing that ever happened to music for a lot of reasons ... I totally got into the whole John and Yoko thing when I was sixteen, seventeen, the whole Plastic Ono Band thing. I loved that and that's made me want to come to Liverpool. Then when I got to Liverpool I remember going to the Cavern club. The original Cavern hadn't shut down and I loved the fact that it was completely empty and there was this metal band, Liverpool metal band but they were all Chinese guys with really long black hair doing cover versions of Status Quo or something and I liked that. I liked the perversion that somehow this is how it ended up. I lived up in Windsor Street in Toxteth, L8, and spent a lot of time going to the African clubs, whether it was the Ebo club, Silver Sands, the Nigeria Club ... the Somali Club and I loved the vibe of those places. On the jukebox in those places [they] had the type of music I was into anyway, they weren't playing African music in there it was mainly American R&B of the day.

IAN BROUDIE: When I was about fourteen we used to come into town and there used to be a warehouse called the Open Mind Warehouse[1] and it was just loads of hippies.... They used to say we could have the gig but we had no singer ... so we used to just jam reggae, we just sort of jammed reggae in E or something for hours and hours and hours and that was our first gig really just doing that.... Mathew Street was, in those days, a really different place you know, because ... you had ice sculptures, big fridges with ice sculptures in them [by Charles Alexander; see Bill Drummond's map in illustration section] and [then] really a lot of waste ground, just kind of a lot of rubble, very run down, nothing much there and it felt like a bit of a forgotten part of town in those days.

STEVE ALLEN: Mathew Street was very run down then; the Cavern had gone, obviously. It had been knocked down and turned into a useless little car park. The main life in the street was O'Halligan's ... and Probe on the corner, Button Street. There was no other shops except a place, a second-hand place, where we used to rummage for stuff in there, really nice shop that sold second-hand antique things you know, and Aunt Twackies, which was second-hand clothes and we used to shop there and buy all our stage stuff. There was nothing much else. O'Halligan's was the centre. That was the focal point of town and that is where we did the Jung Festival organized by [Peter and] Sean O'Halligan [in 1975]. They put a stage in across the bottom of Mathew Street; it was us and Sean who started it and it was because we were such a draw that it could be a successful festival. They had poets on, there were acrobats and we were the top of the bill and it was great … O'Hallagan introduced us to Carl Jung and his dream about Liverpool being the pool of life so that is why he did that statue there. So it was a fantastic point of meeting…. The Armadillo was great; it was the best place to eat in Liverpool because there weren't many other places where you had wholefood stuff … so that was the place and that was the centre, we lived there, every day we were in the Grapes or the Star and so it became [a scene]. Because we were there all the time everyone who wanted to dress up, all the kids who were slight outsiders maybe in Norris Green, they were a bit more sensitive or they were into music, not into football, they would come and be there in the Armadillo café, which was great. It was a very dead time in Liverpool – there was no music; it wasn't like now – loads of bars and restaurants and places to go – there were very few places to go, very few.

Deaf School

STEVE ALLEN: How we started Deaf School was I wanted to do, like, a conceptual art piece, a bit of a theatrical art piece … I wrote the lyrics for a song called 'Cocktails at Eight' and I did that and we filmed it on super eight upstairs at the Philharmonic Cocktail Bar [on Hope Street]. So it was like a little theatrical performance where the head of sculpture [of Liverpool School of Art] played the piano for me in there because there was a piano. My dad used to play piano in there upstairs. It was a really nice little … Edwardian kind of restaurant where they had very good steak pies…. We did a theatrical performance and we filmed it and it was part of my sculpture work, [a] little performance art thing … so that is actually the very first Deaf School song although I didn't have the music.

We were called Deaf School because we rehearsed in the Deaf School, which was in Myrtle Street. It was part of the sculpture department but it wasn't being used much. We borrowed the PA from the art school disco and brought it all in there and we did these rehearsals and we got away with it for ages until one of those real jobsworth little caretakers found out about it…. We were basically the [in-house art] school band and we did a couple of little things like the Christmas party and next thing somebody said there is a pub round the corner called O'Connors Tavern [on Hardman Street] – they have gigs on there…. So the next gig we did was O'Connors Tavern. It was packed full of art school students and they wanted [us back]. It worked from day one…. So we did it again and it was more packed, and we did another one and it was absolutely [rammed], you couldn't get in; we turned up and we could not get in ourselves you know. It was mad. [We thought] 'Something is going on'. Clive [Langer, a member of Deaf School and, later, a highly successful record producer] was like 'Uh, oh, I think we are a band'.

MARTIN DEMPSEY: I came to Liverpool in the early 1970s following a stint at art college in Leeds where I got pretty much involved in performance art with the likes of Welfare State and Genesis P. Orridge in COUM [influential UK performance art movement of the 1970s] so I was very interested in performance.... So being at the art college ... a group of us got together ostensibly to be a performing arts outfit ... and we started off by borrowing their [Deaf School's] equipment to rehearse with. Deaf School were quite unusual in [that] they were a very theatrical band but were very stylish and stylized, obviously influenced by the likes of David Bowie and that kind of thing but obviously more like Jacques Brel and the kind of more eccentric songwriter things. The musicianship was quite well developed but yet they also had a tendency to go into more bizarre things.... The art college was very influential in what was going on.... There was nothing very alternative. O'Connors was a fairly run-down serious drinking haunt that did a bit of folk music but then they decided, because the Art College people used to drink there, to put Deaf School on. Then we [Albert Dock and the Cod Warriors] got to play there and another band who were quite interesting at the time were a band called Nasty Pop. They did an album [released in 1975] and did okay briefly. The rest of what was going on was kind of, that kind of early '70s progressive rock really, some of it being done very well but it wasn't cutting edge and it was mainly people doing cover stuff.

STEVE ALLEN: We had to go and search for other places to play in. There weren't many so we opened our own venue called the Back of the Moon, off Bold Street. We knew a place that was kind of empty and the guy was closing it down but he had a few months to run on his lease and we said, 'Well, can we play here?'... We did our own posters in the art school ... kind of kitsch, very arty and so that obviously attracted those kind of people [but also an audience] from the normal Liverpool, which is this weird thing. Liverpool bridges this gap between arty art school students and normal Liverpool kids who like music and it was interesting, you know. So we put the posters around town. We could hardly move in the Back of the Moon for the first gig.

NORMAN KILLON: [Deaf School] really kick started live music again in Liverpool. It was really moribund by then. There was music going on in pubs but they were doing things like Led Zeppelin songs or

Steppenwolf songs. It wasn't anything really new or interesting. There were a lot of people who took Deaf School to their hearts; they had a huge following in Liverpool.

Eric's

IAN BROUDIE: It wasn't called Eric's: it was called the Revolution first, and I remember, I think, it was a band called the Runaways were on and I was quite interested in Kim Fowley because he was kind of a weird, Phil Spector-type producer and Kim Fowley had discovered the Runaways. I remember calling for one of my mates and we sort of snuck into town and queued up outside and went in to see the Runaways ... and then out of that Eric's kind of formed. I think it was the same place but it went downstairs.

MARTIN DEMPSEY: Roger Eagle had been running a place called the Stadium and they managed to rent a Thursday evening at a club in town which was called Gatsby's. The upstairs part of Gatsby's was where the first few gigs of Eric's happened. The main band played before eleven o'clock upstairs and then after midnight you could go downstairs into the basement where the support band played. So we played it as Albert Dock and the Cod Warriors with the Sex Pistols. That went on for about six weeks and they managed to get a hold of the licence to run downstairs so that is when they named it Eric's. It became a club night on a Thursday and Saturday at first and then it became practically every night of the week, running evening and [with] matinees for younger people in the day time.

STEVE ALLEN: Ken Testi, who had been our tour manager, basically started Eric's. It was '76, and we did the first gig when they had the upstairs bit, not the downstairs bit. There was an upstairs bit of Eric's; Deaf School did the first gig then, not the Pistols, as they always put in the biog: we did the first show.

NORMAN KILLON: The first act [Roger Eagle] had on was the Runaways. There had been a buzz around them just prior to that so he really lucked out. There were crash barriers all around Mathew Street. It was a complete sell-out, so loads of people didn't get into that one. Then they had the Sex Pistols and the Stranglers and then they moved downstairs.

PETE FULWELL: It was [a] dark, dingy, classic rock club, black everywhere, flashes of red. Toilets were abominable. It seemed to me it was a cellar in what was once an underground stream so that whenever it rained the club would flood, literally flood. I remember being down there one afternoon and there was a massive street festival going on, which in those days was more about performance art and quite small, and I went down into the club because it was raining heavily and I knew that the water was going to start coming up through the toilets. There was like a grid there, so I went down and sure enough it was just starting to seep out, so I stood on it trying to call out through the window to let people know that I was there and I was stuck on this thing. The water was pressing up and I couldn't move so in the end I literally had to shrug and step off it. Whoosh! There was no gig that night. We had to get the pumps down and the driers. So it was very much about suffering in the cause of rock and roll really. People used to say it was like CBGBs [the centre of New York punk rock] and years later when I was managing I went there and I could see what they meant. Its reputation was much bigger, not unlike Liverpool in many ways; it was boxing way above its weight. As for atmosphere, it depended on what night you were talking about. If it was a band that people wanted to see it was heaving and literally a bit like the Cavern: condensation dripping off the walls and all the rest of it. But if it was a band, even though it might be significant, that people weren't interested in, it was a bit like a morgue; there might be twenty or thirty people there usually amongst the regulars who would go to everything because they didn't have to pay to get in and they didn't have to pay to get any drinks which is one of the reasons why we went bust. It was all a bit chaotic but great fun.

HILARY STEELE: All the bands were very accessible. There was a dressing room in Eric's but you had to walk through the club to get to the stage and the dressing room as pretty grotty anyway so no one stayed there very long.

Roger Eagle

PETE FULWELL: Oh he was lovely. He was one of those larger-than-life people and I am sure he would be amused at the way he has been kind of transformed into a mythological figure now.... He was one of nature's educators. He was passionate about music, particularly R&B, and would insist on educating you with it. Very, very passionate about it, a born showman, a promoter, loved to be the host, loved to be standing at the door welcoming people and so on. He also liked the power that went with it but was pretty hopeless when it came to money and stuff like that and the mechanics of making things happen, so to a certain extent, you know, Ken and I complemented that. But Roger, as I say, he was a larger-than-life character, passionate about music and I miss him; very rarely a week goes by without having a conversation with him actually.

STEVE ALLEN: Roger Eagle was a legend. He was fantastic from being the DJ at the Twisted Wheel in Manchester, doing the northern soul stuff. This guy lived and breathed everything about music; his record collection was amazing. He introduced us to dub reggae before the Clash.... He was playing all that sort of stuff down at Eric's, great music taste. There was only ever good music on in Eric's ... and a good crowd of kids and somewhere to go again because there weren't any other places.

IAN BROUDIE: Roger was a real character, you know. The first time I ever went to Eric's I think we ended up talking to Roger. I think he talked to everyone who went in there, told them they were wearing the wrong thing, [that they] didn't know anything about music and [had] better listen to this.... Thinking about it now, I was like this little lad hanging about that club and he had these fantastic records. He'd been a DJ in the '60s and had a really wide collection of rare records and stuff and he used to lend me them and let me take them home and I'd take a couple and then I'd bring them back and he'd give me something else and it was really quite an education in music, you know, it was stuff that I'd never heard before and that was ... a massive thing for me really.

Eric's as a creative scene

HILARY STEELE: There wasn't anything. I had this love of Bowie and Roxy [Music] but by then [they] were massive. Of course you could go and see them but I just couldn't find a small scene. By then I was almost about to give up college 'cos I thought 'Well Liverpool, I can't really connect very much'. [But when I went to Eric's] I just thought 'Yes this is it, I've found it.' We went to Eric's and it was a midweek night. It was the Yachts so it wasn't some mad punk band but I thought finally I've found what I'd been looking for [for] a year.... I felt finally I'm at home now, I've found something that I can connect with.

JAYNE CASEY: Eric's opening was the most incredible thing in the world to us. It totally, totally changed our lives you know. I remember the day that I was in my store [Aunt Twackies] and this big guy came bumbling in and said 'I'm opening a club and I want you and your mates to come to it'. And he handed me these tickets and it was such a shock because nobody wanted you to go to their club! You know, they were all terrified of the trouble that would emerge if you went into their club. So it was really strange to be invited to their club and it was Roger Eagle and it was the opening night of Eric's. It totally altered everything for us, Eric's. It gave us a home from the first day we walked in there. We never paid to get in. Roger knew that to create a scene he needed cutting-edge kids of a similar movement to what was going on in London or whatever. He kind of eyeballed us and thought, you know, I need those kind of people in my club.

PETE FULWELL: I think there was an element … of social engineering going on, as there was at any club. You want to have a club that opinion leaders go to because the followers will follow them…. In spite of appearances, it wasn't a club where there was a strong vision that was imposed on the club and people followed it. It was very much shaped by that kind of hard-core of people that came regularly and their views on what they thought it should be; they didn't actually have committees or anything like that but it was much more democratic and responsive to that than perhaps the reputation.

MARTIN DEMPSEY: [Eric's] was very, very influential in the whole of Liverpool's street ethic and dress and fashion and design and everything else because it broke the mould. I am not saying it is just because of the art students but I am sure that was a big influence because the art students include the fashion students, the design students, etc. not just from the Art College from the other surrounding colleges further afield. So you would have people coming over from Wales, you would have people come from Chester, you would have people coming from Manchester into the club because they knew, or they heard, that it was a safe place to come. And then mini-buses and coaches started coming and it was a safe place for people to develop their … own imagination. So cross-dressing and gay things and transvestism. All could go there and not get hassled.

IAN BROUDIE: Arty I'd describe it as. I think there were a lot of people who used to go there and it was the idea of it as much as the music. It was its own little world really. You'd get to see bands … but also it was like a refuge for kind of, outcasts to a certain extent. It was a lot of weird-looking people … you might not otherwise have run into and it was always very friendly. You'd always be just chatting to a lot of different people, so it was somewhere that you could go down on your own and be talking to loads of people throughout the night. It didn't feel like clubs feel now really … and it felt like everyone shared a bit of an obsession for being a bit different and maybe music and trying to make a mark really…. I used to DJ a bit in there and load in and out for the groups. So I'd be there, load the amps in, every now and again on a quiet night might DJ a bit, load the amps out, and it became a bit of the centre of my universe really. The group I was in, Big in Japan – we used to rehearse there, so we'd sort of be in there in the afternoon rehearsing, then we'd stop rehearsing when the group that were playing that night arrived, load the gear in, get a fiver for loading the gear in, hang about, you know, maybe DJ for another fiver and then hang about till it was all finished and load it out sometimes. So a lot of my days were spent in Mathew Street doing that.

PETE FULWELL: In terms of the atmosphere it was very, very Art College centred, Deaf School centred. They played a big part in the original initial culture and there were bands like Big in Japan who formed out of the roadies and they would be down the club a lot. There was another band called Yachts which were a bunch of guys from art school. Those guys were all part of the initial shaping of it, mixed in with alienated, young, working class, punks. Quite a heavy mixture really.

NORMAN KILLON: [After Eric's opened] it was kind of a scene where we were. 'Cos there was Probe on the corner and there was Extremes [a clothes shop] a bit further up and then there was Aunt Twackies, which was a bazaar with loads of stalls, and Jayne Casey had a stall there. So it kind of created its own scene. A lot of people's musical tastes were encapsulated by Probe; they would come in and find out about things they didn't know about.... If you knew somebody and they came in, you'd say 'Have you heard this?' and you'd put it on. Of course we had people [working in the shop] who became famous, Paul Rutherford and Holly [Johnson], Pete Burns, Pete Wylie, Mac [Ian McCulloch]: they all had a turn behind the counter until they got bored.

Forming bands

JAYNE CASEY: One day in my stall in Aunt Twackies a man came in and started freaking out when he saw me.... I had a shaved head and eye make-up on which was a little bit pyramid shaped. He kept saying 'Oh my god it's the eye of the pyramid' and I thought 'You're mad!' He was Ken Campbell, the theatre director, and he'd been in Liverpool for a visit to the Everyman theatre because he'd got the rights to produce a play based on a trilogy of books by Robert Anton Wilson called *The Illuminati*. I don't think the meeting at the Everyman went very well and before he got his train home he'd walked down Mathew Street and dropped into my stall and he decided he wanted to put on his play in that building because the sign of the Illuminati was an eye in the pyramid and I had an eye in the pyramid. He moved into the building using the café upstairs and he brought loads of the London scene; Keith Allen and Chris Langham [actors] and loads of different people. He wanted me to be the singer in the play but I'd say 'I really can't sing' … and Bill Drummond was set designer of the *Illuminati*, Ian Broudie was the guitarist in the band and Budgie was the drummer in the band. So I never sang but I was in the play and we all became friends. So suddenly the little scene was expanding so there's Pete Burns, Holly [Johnson], Paul Rutherford and Bill and Ian Broudie. After the play was finished Bill decided he wanted to put a band together. So that's how Big in Japan formed. It was through Ken Campbell's *Illuminati*.

DAVID LITTLER OF THE BAND THE SPITFIRE BOYS: It was early in '77, about March I think, that I saw the Heartbreakers at Eric's and spoke to them after the gig. I told them I had a group called the Blackmailers (which I didn't) and they offered us a support slot at Warrington Parr Hall with Slaughter and the Dogs and the Buzzcocks in May. This gave me about five or six weeks to put the band together. We had a friend called Mike Rigby, who offered to sing, and we loaned a drummer from a local rock band. I gave Peter Griffiths my brother's bass guitar and showed him the notes to play, and with me on guitar we rehearsed in Mike Rigby's garage.… I met Wayne County [US punk singer with the Electric Chairs] and asked him a good name for a band as I wasn't happy with the Blackmailers; it was his suggestion, the Spitfire Boys, and it stuck.[2]

CLIVE LANGER: I used to jam with … Big In Japan, which was formed in 1977 out of the Deaf School road crew. Various line-ups included Holly Johnson on bass, Bill Drummond on guitar, Budgie on drums and Dave Balfe [later of the Teardrop Explodes] on bass. The Crucial Three [a legendary band of the period, who never got as far as playing gigs, comprising Julian Cope, Ian McCulloch and Pete Wylie] also came [out of the Eric's scene].… Julian went on to form the Teardrop Explodes, Ian McCulloch joined Echo and the Bunnymen and Pete Wylie formed Wah! So it was very exciting up there, but it took a few years for the Liverpool bands to break through. (Quoted in Colgrave and Sullivan 2001: 356)

IAN BROUDIE: The thing that made me actually believe that I might be able to do it was punk rock really.… When I was about sixteen, seventeen, I started going to Probe Records. The Ramones were a massive influence. The Ramones made me rethink everything, throw out all my albums.… A lot of the New York bands really, Television, the Ramones, Patti Smith, Talking Heads, you know they'd just had their first single out I think, 'Love Goes to a Building on Fire'. And then of course Eric's was open so we were actually seeing these bands pretty quickly.... It was a place to go and it was certainly a place where you met like-minded people and a lot of the bands formed out of the friendships that people made there so … it inspired people to form bands.

BILL DRUMMOND: I'd seen the Clash [at Eric's] on the same night as we formed Big in Japan … and they were stunning and it really, really invigorated my belief, you know, that rock music can work, you know, four guys – the whole cliché can work.

WILL SERGEANT, OF ECHO AND THE BUNNYMEN: I used to work as a trainee chef in a large department store in the centre of Liverpool.... I worked there for about five years. The Bunnymen only overlapped this time by a few months. We were just starting to get gigs in London and I would be getting back to Liverpool at about 7 a.m., then going straight to work. It was obvious I had to leave, so I did. The people there thought I was mad to give up a job to start a band.... But I do think without this job in the centre of town I would never have been exposed to the club scene in Liverpool. The store was just around the corner from Eric's. Somehow it became apparent to me that there were these weirdos hanging out down Mathew Street and Probe Records – which was my lunchtime haunt. I went on my own and was completely entranced by the punk scene. (Quoted in Hanson 2001)

PETE WYLIE, OF WAH HEAT! AND THE MIGHTY WAH!: I met Julian [Cope] because he was dancing right in front of me [at the Clash gig]. He was really pissing me off 'cos he kept dancing into me. I was nudging him to stop and he was ignoring me. We ended up talking and we decided to form a band. We didn't even know if the other could play. (Quoted in Cooper 1982: 20–21)

JULIAN COPE, OF THE TEARDROP EXPLODES: We met in a bunch. Everyone was very quiet, walking round each other to find out if they were into the right things.... After that night, Wylie, Mac and I formed the Crucial Three. Even then we were into being a legend, hence the name. We had about four songs and about four rehearsals.... All three of us wanted to be the lead singer but Mac couldn't play anything so he had to be the singer. (Quoted in Cooper 1982: 21)

HILARY STEELE: Suddenly, everybody was getting up and being in a band. It was like, 'Yeah I'll have a go anyway'. And someone like Mac. It was amazing. He was such a quiet person. He'd been around for about a year and suddenly he got up and was in a band and he'd just got this amazing voice, which kind of shocked everyone. I was like,

CHAPTER 8

Dance moves: finding a place for house music in Liverpool

Georgina Young

Introduction

This chapter considers the relationship of house music to Liverpool and the uneasy relationship of this musical style to place. The idea of place, specifically the city of Liverpool in this case study, sits uneasily with house music. There is no simple equation (Liverpool = house music capital) or grand narrative (house music finds its home in Liverpool) that ties the city and house music together. Nevertheless, the emergence of a vibrant club culture within the city has played an important part in the city's cultural life, contemporary image, night-time economy and strategies for urban regeneration over the past twenty years. Clubs such as Voodoo, Garlands and Chibuku have become some of the most celebrated and well known in the country, while Cream has transcended its roots as a club night to become a well known entertainment brand. The chapter thus uses a number of case studies in order to trace the emergence of the post-acid-house club scene within the city, with specific reference to its changing relationship to the city's geography and culture.

House music

House music is a form of electronic dance music characterized by a mosaic structure made up of a variety of looped samples, synthesizer lines and electronic effects grounded by a prominent repetitive beat. It started in the US cities of Chicago, Detroit and New York in the late 1970s and early 1980s before becoming associated with the nightclubs and beach parties of the Balearic islands off the east coast of Spain and making a huge impact through open-air and warehouse parties across the UK in the late 1980s during the 'Second Summer of Love'. At this stage the scene was incredibly mobile and unified not by place but by the transient ecstatic communal experiences of those involved. This poses some problems for a chapter looking at notions of place and how they might be connected to the house music scene. Striving to tie the scene down to a comprehensive series of locations where house music has been played in Liverpool and Merseyside would be both near impossible and near meaningless. Moreover, in studying club cultures there are inherent methodological problems in mapping and explaining, over and above experiencing and participating. When meaning is made in the moment, enervated by the music and shared by the audience, what can a grid reference tell you?[1] The formations of place relevant to the Liverpool and Merseyside house scene are more complex and more malleable than physical description alone allows.

It is not possible to characterize the house scene in Liverpool in the same way as Merseybeat or post-punk, key antecedent scenes that made an international impact. The making of house music in the city is for the most part not exceptional, personality driven or significant in terms of the way the scene is narrated; there is no house equivalent of the Beatles. House venues have rarely assumed the gravity or mythical quality of other venues such as Eric's, the club that brought a series of big-name punk bands to Liverpool and nurtured an audience including future members of Frankie Goes to Hollywood and Echo and the Bunnymen (see chapter 7). Indeed, it could be argued that Cream's home venue – Nation – became almost irrelevant, as the club night transcended its origins through its evolution into a global brand attached to mix CDs, merchandise and a series of club nights and festivals across Europe, the United States, South America and Australia. Nevertheless, the house scene in Liverpool is remarkable on its own terms and its club culture is distinct. This distinction comes largely from the nature of the music around which the scene is based. House tends not to have regionally accented vocal lines or place-referencing lyrics and the strengths of individual tracks take precedence over the bodies of work of identifiable musicians. House music becomes specific and local in the way that it is reassembled by DJs and consumed by its communities in the moment. The very malleability and (in traditional terms) placelessness of the music becomes a strength:

> house records are not recordings 'of' performances, they are actively 'performed' by the DJ himself, allowing spontaneity, surprise and creativity. It is this direct and reciprocal relationship between the DJ and his audience that makes a rave[2] a qualitatively 'special' event and allows the participants to become emotionally involved in the music. (Langlois 1992: 236)

This chapter does not try to definitively resolve the relationship between Liverpool and house music or to plot house venues on a map. Rather, it a series of sketches of different moments in the history of house music in Liverpool, each of which highlights different aspects of the way in which the house scene has interacted with the idea of place and the city of Liverpool.

Do you remember the first time?

When house first exploded across the UK in 1987 and 1988 it was always moving, never fixed to one club or place. People met up at weekend open-air raves, warehouse parties and one-off events. Where was your first rave? In a field near Blackburn? Somewhere off the M25? A dockside warehouse? 'No idea, in a field, somewhere, near Chorley someone said later' (Andy Carroll, oral history). Liverpool doesn't often feature in local participants' narratives of early acid-house parties; there are few details of places at all.

To an extent, the specific field or warehouse did not matter as it bore little relation to the experience of being there. Various critics have articulated the nature of this experience as being transcendent or transformative in terms of space. Langlois (1992: 236) argues that house events 'generate a "liminal" existence, ritually separating, by various means, the ordinary world from the dance environment'. Similarly, Ingham (1999) situates the Blackburn raves of the late 1980s in 'temporary autonomous zones' in which the restrictions of space were momentarily transcended. Empathogenic drugs like ecstasy and the structures of house music act to heighten the transcendent effect: 'The lengthy repetition of a single rhythm is considered a very important component in the creation of the desired "other worldly" ambience. In performance it maintains the atmosphere of temporal distortion created in many clubs' (Langois 1992: 235). Anthropological literature around dance as 'communitas' (Spencer 1985) and references in pop culture to a higher state of consciousness[3] both identify moments within the house movement that are placeless. As Fikentscher (2000: 75) notes, the audiovisual conventions of the rave are 'apt, even designed to lead to other-than-everyday sensations on the part of the dancer', in turn leading to the 'manifestation of possibility, the option, or the attempt to step outside the restrictions, conventions, and norms of the world beyond the doors of the dance venue'.

Early house events were often organized outside of established club environments, in unlicensed, semi-derelict buildings or wide open spaces with few identifiable features. The location of parties was disclosed by phone at the last minute and went largely unrecorded on flyers or other documents. There were certainly open-air parties within the city of Liverpool and its surrounds, some of which are recalled in relation to totemic Merseyside places by James Barton in his oral history:

> It was a real scene of people just going from one place to the next. One week there'd be a party on Crosby beach and there'd be two thousand people there and then there'd be something going off in Sefton Park a day later and there'd be three thousand people there … it really felt like the beginning of a musical revolution.

Although Barton identifies some known areas of activity, many of the places where parties happened are now forgotten or hard to relocate. Abandoned Liverpool warehouses, in part because there were so many, are some of the less placeable of the early party sites in the city. Even local house DJs like Andy Carroll sometimes struggled to get a fix on what was happening where:

As DJs we'd be like, 'Well, c'mon lads, tell us beforehand where these parties are gonna be' and they'd just sort of say nothing and years later I found out that the reason that no one could tell us or would was because they actually didn't know. The moment the bush telegraph got the phone call was the moment that they'd got into a warehouse quite simply.... I did a warehouse party round Liverpool; all I can tell you is, it was probably in the area of where the New Picket is, if you know where that is, round Jamaica Street. It was probably round there somewhere.

Carroll could be referring to any one of dozens of warehouses set back from the docks to the south of the city centre. There is a kind of folklore around the place of house on Merseyside whenever it is disassociated from traditional licensed club-land, a series of loose ends trailing from the imaginations of those who were there. There was a house scene in the city right from the start, but it remains an intangible heritage because the participants' memories of place are centred on the experience of 'being there' rather than precisely where they were geographically.

The state we're in

The use of abandoned spaces and outdoor locations arose partly from the fact that Liverpool's established clubs were slow on the uptake in terms of dance music. The first shoots of Liverpool city centre's distinctive house scene emerged in late 1988. Bits and pieces of house music had been mixed with indie dance by braver DJs in places like the Pyramid club on Temple Street, near Moorfields station, but there was nothing in Liverpool's urban club-land that could rival the itinerant open-air raves and warehouse parties of the Second Summer of Love. It took a determined effort by a young James Barton to bring Liverpool its first house night, Daisy, at the State Ballroom on Dale Street, in the city's business district:

It was summer 1988 and there were impromptu parties going off in places like Sefton Park, in little tiny warehouses and stuff like that, the beginnings, little tiny things. But then I'd already arranged with Bernie Start, who owned the State back then, that I would do a deal with him – the club was never open on a Monday – and I would do a Monday-night dance night, which we started on September the 12th

1988, and it was called Daisy and the whole theme of it was acid house and Balearic beats, which was quite funny, and that was the first – as far as I'm aware – it was the first Liverpool dance night: first proper dance night inside a nightclub in Liverpool.

At the time when Daisy secured this foothold, the State was an icon of the Liverpool alternative music scene. It had evolved from a ballroom through several incarnations into a popular, if unglamorous, alternative dance venue. It was in the business district and a little way from Liverpool club-land, as Paul Du Noyer characterizes it:

> Liverpool nightlife has always had an edgy quality. Traditional Liverpool club-land was a gorgeously seedy place, full of corruption, sporadically violent, always loud. By day the district was dull, like factory overalls, but after dark it turned itself inside out, to become a suit of lights. (Du Noyer 2007: 207)

It's a matter of faith whether you believe in Du Noyer's poetic thesis on Liverpool as a 'wondrous place', always entertaining, always poised to party. There were certainly socio-economic factors that made the city fertile ground for house music in the late 1980s. Like other northern towns and cities, Liverpool suffered during the 1980s, but, over a longer span, its decline was exceptional, as it went from being one of the richest cities in the world to one of the poorest in Europe. Liverpool's population was dwindling, its unemployment – its poverty – soaring. The *Changing City* report (Social and Spatial Inequalities Group 2008) showed that Merseyside's population fell faster and further between 1981 and 2006 than anywhere else in England, collapsing by 6.8 per cent. Similarly, the 1980 *Merseyside in Crisis* report stated that:

> Unemployment levels have invariably been twice the national average ... but over the last few years the rate of unemployment in the Merseyside area has risen to such an extent that by 1978 it was 11.7%, the highest in England. This year [1980] it is 12.3% – 100,000 people out of work. (Merseyside Socialist Research Group 1980: 10)

The docks – the source of unseemly wealth and mass employment a century before – had moved north, mechanized and containerized, and become detached from the heart of the city, leaving a trail of dereliction behind them. The fabric of the place was full of holes where workplaces had once been and Liverpool's people were a ready market for 'temporal distortion' and 'other worldly ambience'. Even so, the appetite of Liverpool for a regular house night wasn't immediately evident at the time, according to Mike Knowler, one of the resident DJs, in his oral history:

> The first one [Daisy], we opened our doors at nine o'clock and by half past ten there was nobody in and we just thought, 'Oh, this is not going to happen; Liverpool isn't ready for acid house', and then about quarter to eleven people streamed in and by half eleven the place was rammed and I just couldn't believe it. That night ran for something like ten weeks, but while it was happening the crowd that were coming on a Monday came back on a Friday and a Saturday – or a Thursday, Friday and a Saturday – and the result is that they arrived in such numbers that they forced out the Goths and the Rockabillies and the indie crowd – the Smiths fans – and by the Christmas of 1988 the State Ballroom was 100 per cent acid house.

James Barton, Mike Knowler and Mike's fellow resident DJ Andy Carroll had hit a nerve and set a transformation in motion: 'that building was never the same again! In fact the city just didn't seem to be the same again; everywhere you went everybody wanted house music' (Andy Carroll). Having temporarily altered the State (Daisy lasted only a matter of weeks), James Barton rapidly followed Liverpool's first house night with Liverpool's first house club, the Underground, on nearby Victoria Street, which had a longer and deeper impact. Meanwhile, like minds were doing their own thing. DJ John Kelly and Peter Coyle (formerly of indie band the Lotus Eaters) promoted a much-loved Thursday night soulful funky house club called G-Love at the Mardi Gras on Bold Street, while student venue McMillan's on Concert Square took a progressive angle. Most individual house nights and clubs in central Liverpool in the late 1980s and early 1990s were transitory by nature or short-lived, as the scene was hounded from place to place by a series of police raids and revoked licences. On 18 June 1990, Martin Wainwright filed one of a series of acid house raid reports for the *Guardian*:

> Three people were arrested in Liverpool early yesterday after an acid house party attended by 400 ended peacefully at 5 a.m. in a disused warehouse off Derby Road. The arrests were for suspicion of possessing drugs, possessing an offensive weapon and theft. (Wainwright 1990a)[4]

Media reports like these reflected and generated anxiety around 'acid house', but despite the resultant interventions by city authorities and rapid turnover of venues, the Liverpool house audience was not going anywhere. Well, maybe to Bootle....

Out-of-towners

In the metropolitan borough of Sefton, to the north of Liverpool, near to the dock road, among the industrial estates, on a five-acre warehouse site, Quadrant Park helped to define house on Merseyside from a less-than-promising position. Quadrant Park, better known as the Quad to its patrons, had been a lack-lustre disco club and twenty-four-hour snooker hall before the introduction of house music at the end of 1989. Early house events were DJed by Mike Knowler, who had established a reputation at the State and carried a dedicated audience with him. The frequency and popularity of house nights at the Quad increased during 1990 and the venue's dislocation became part of its mythology. Where better to create a sense of abandon than in an area itself abandoned? The journey to get there, the struggle to work out which of the shabby warehouses was the right one and the disorientation the next morning all generated a sense of adventure and otherness. Even for people living in the area, 'It was very odd. I knew people who came up from London for it. I could walk home in ten minutes. But afterwards you'd see all these people, really wrecked, going, "How do we get home from Bootle?"' (Kevin McManus, quoted in Du Noyer 2007: 215).

Once you got there, the audience at the Quad was sweaty, smiley and hands-in-the-air. They went some way to explaining the magnetic quality of the place, why the atmosphere and experience were special, as described by 'Left Side' on a web forum:

> Walking onto that dance floor – you could almost smell it – something's different here. And then a tune kicked in and the place went into one. 'Christ, what is this?' I thought. Airhorns, cheers, huge grins and people going absolutely mental – I drew breath and then was straight into it – hooked and loving every minute.[5]

In some ways Left Side could be describing any club, but by posting on the forum of www.quadrantpark.com, 'the home of

Quadrant Park nostalgia', he places himself and his visceral, over-whelming experience within both a location and a community. The website was established by Quadrant Park clubber turned house DJ Ian Kenyon in 2002 and its forum followed in 2005. The active use of both to share Quad pictures and tales indicates just how significant the experience of attending the club was to those who were there and just how fiercely they identify with that remembered place. The forum includes a thread entitled 'WHERE WAS UR AREA IN QUAD??', where locations and communities become even more specific. With 77 replies and 2,414 views, it is by far the most viewed and contributed to discussion strand, virtually recreating the club floor by floor and face by face. The Quad warehouse was demolished years ago with little protest and is all but forgotten in terms of the manifest built environment, but its house community is still very much intact and individual members recall the interior space with great accuracy, identifying themselves not just with the club but with specific locations within it. Resident DJ Mike Knowler is precise in his recollections of the Quad and clear on its significance for Liverpool:

> I think the significance of Quadrant Park to Liverpool is that, unlike the State, which only really catered to people from Liverpool or at the very most the odd person from Warrington or Chester, Quadrant Park attracted people from all over the country and the reason was because from November 1990 through until August of 1991 we had probably the only weekly, legal, all-night rave in the country. It held about 5,000 people in a warehouse and an entertainment licence that had been granted for a twenty-four-hour snooker club was manipulated, for want of a better word, so it could be used to allow us to run an all-night rave; the condition of this was that it was members only.

The paradox of Quadrant Park (not to be confused with Paradox – another famed house club beyond the north of the city centre) was that it was open to all, while technically being a members-only club. The 'no dress restrictions' slogan on Quadrant Park flyers reflected its democratic door policy, but in order to put on the 'genuine rave' the publicity also promised, it had to operate as a private members' club. Skipping the requirement for a public entertainment licence, the Quad could open all night and avoid strict controls on noise and crowds. A membership card was a ticket to dancing all through the night. This unique selling point helped Quadrant Park attract audiences from beyond its Merseyside heartland and gave the Liverpool house scene a national profile for the first time:

> MIKE KNOWLER: [The all-nighter] became a national phenomenon; there were coaches coming from as far as Aberdeen to that, people coming up from London, all over the place. It was probably one of the first legal all-nighters – in Bootle – there it was – brilliant!

During 1991, however, the tide of the Liverpool house scene started to turn away from Quadrant Park. As the club's profile went up, so did the price of entry, along with the amount of attention it received from council authorities, police and local gangsters. The Quad's atmosphere changed and as a consequence its original audience gradually ebbed away. Without the people who had made the place their own, Quadrant Park closed down in January 1992.

Dance palaces

As the Quad's popularity waned, city-centre club-land was stirring again and pulling house back into the heart of Liverpool. The Academy on Wolstenholme Square established itself as a house venue, with nights like Eden; regular club nights like Paul Kane's Smile night at Rio's on Seel Street gained dedicated crowds; and the Ofiveone made a fleeting attempt to become Liverpool's version of Manchester's ground-breaking Hacienda club. The Ofiveone even asserted its central Liverpool identity in its name – a reference to the telephone area code for the city at the time – to define itself as a destination and once again to re-articulate the malleable and perpetually reconstructed house music form in relation to Liverpool. This use of Liverpool identity to position and market a house club foreshadowed the later co-option of house-scene brands by city authorities to market the city.

Beyond the Ofiveone, a hive of house activity was forming, stretching through the semi-derelict, criss-crossing, warehouse-lined streets running back into town from Paradise Street and Park Lane and centring on the Duke Street/Bold Street area. James Barton describes how it felt from his position inside the Liverpool Palace on Slater Street:

Liverpool at that beginning, probably '91–92, was just going through its first phase of regeneration. Suddenly we were getting a couple of style bars, a couple of little restaurants and we had this little, thriving, tiny dance music industry going on up at the Liverpool Palace. There was 3 Beat Records in there, there was us in there, there was Rob Swerdlow who managed the La's at the time, and then suddenly the Farm came on the scene and we were all mates and we'd all hang out together and I used to DJ with the Farm and stuff. You know, the whole thing was like this little four or five offices in one building where we were all involved in our own way in dance music.

The Palace was a place where house mixed with other music genres, where the record-hungry bought the latest imports from the 3 Beat Records shop, where a genuinely inclusive scene coalesced and where Liverpool's definitive house club, Cream, was masterminded. It was also in the streets around the Palace, as Barton indicates, that house music crossed paths with the urban regeneration agenda in Liverpool. The Duke Street/Bold Street area had first been framed as a 'cultural district' in a 1989 report for the city council, but up until the mid-1990s a series of schemes aimed at regenerating the area as a 'cultural quarter' failed to get beyond the consultation stages. By this time the house scene had made these streets its own.

James Barton started Cream with Darren Hughes and Andy Carroll towards the end of 1992, in the back room of Liverpool Academy on Wolstenholme Square, later known as the Nation Annexe. It was a weekly house-music night that had something special. Part of its initial specialness was an authenticity borrowed from the great cities of American house: New York, Chicago and Detroit. Cream evoked them through its music selection and back-to-basics approach, in order to recapture the early sense of excitement around the first imports of house music and to re-form Liverpool's house community anew. Cream also borrowed something of Liverpool – its reputation as a party city – to establish its reputation. These early halcyon days of pure house partying evolved into Liverpool's defining super-club. Cream's loyal crowd outgrew the back room of the Academy and the club took ownership of the whole venue over time, renaming it Nation and adding the 1,300-capacity Courtyard to the existing 1,000-capacity main room and 700-capacity annexe. As it grew physically, it increased its DJ muscle, and attracted some of the biggest superstar DJs of the mid-1990s. With 2,000 packing out the space each Saturday and following resident DJ Paul Oakenfold's every beat, Cream at its peak was the place to be seen for its high-fashion, high-energy community of Liverpool regulars and a landmark night for the clubbers who came from far and wide to experience a night there.

At the same time, a new hybrid of pub and club was taking shape a few streets away. Baa Bar opened in 1991, backed by property development company Urban Splash, and was looking to establish a new audience. Baa Bar identified a gap between a traditional pub and a club in Liverpool and set about filling it with its winning combination of drinks promotions, modern design and a chart house music sound-track, in the process helping to establish a model that would be echoed in every town centre in the land. Capitalizing on the success of Baa Bar, Urban Splash turned the run-down buildings around Concert Square into ready spaces for national chains like Walkabout and Lloyds Bar to follow its lead. A new pattern was being established for a night out, with the next generation of clubbers journeying through a series of pre-club venues, including Cream's own Mello Mello, before queuing round the block in Wolstenholme Square and flooding the Cream dance floor. Cream was actively involved in the regeneration of Rope Walks, as the Duke Street/Bold Street area was renamed in 1998 (Gilmore 2004: 118), but the super-club's engagement masked a conflict between the house scene's idea of place and that espoused by development agencies. As Gilmore puts it:

[Popular music] creates problems for urban regeneration, through its evolving, dynamic and elusive qualities which prove hard to capture and relate to initiative geared to improving public realm and built environment, through its audibility and its potential to disrupt public space, and through its ties to youth culture, risk, rebellion and disorder. (Gilmore 2004: 110)

The cyclic re-formations of house communities and house places were being muscled out by an altogether more physical, fixed definition of place, concerned with street furniture and paving materials in the Rope Walks. On the ground this was felt keenly as a loss of freedom and authenticity by first-generation ravers:

It all seemed to go a bit corporate with the advance of Cream and the Quad and stuff like that; it turned into a bit of a factory ... all the open-air things all kind of fizzled out as well at the same time, like the Larks in the Park and Groundbeat and all that.[6]

Many in the scene deeply resented Cream's size and slickness over-riding the smaller initiatives and the do-it-yourself openness of the early days.

Out of place

James Barton had a lot to do with the innovative transitions from place to place of Liverpool's house scene and the scene's renown beyond the city is intrinsically linked to his entrepreneurial talent and the resultant global success of Cream. For him, the ideal of Cream was disjointed from its physical environment from the start:

> Initially, we couldn't think of a good name to come up with and I'd had this name in my head for something for a few months, but wasn't quite sure whether we should call it this, but then I said, 'Well, you know, I've got a name, why don't we call it Cream?', and there was some discussion about that and the discussion about that around that time was well, is it clubby? Is it this? Is it that? But I think we all really liked the name and the way it sounded. It was a bit presumptu-ous for us to call a night Cream when cream for me invokes themes of quality and pureness and whatever, when it was a real shit-hole and there was water running down one side of the wall, the toilets were a mess and everything else; it sort of didn't fit the name but we went with it and it stuck and Cream opened on October 12th 1992.

Early on, Cream realized the value of marketing itself as a brand. The distinctive three-lobed logo appeared on publicity and merchan-dise, while glossy marketing campaigns built up awareness of Cream beyond the house scene. The disjunction between the Cream brand and the basic physical reality of Nation that James Barton describes didn't seem to matter all that much to the audience; for a time, Nation and Cream became interchangeable, one and the same thing in the eyes of clubbers. The distinction (and likewise the less than salubrious built environment) was secondary to what that place meant to them in the moment, experiencing the music as part of a community. Respected local dance music website Outlar still lists Nation as 'Nation AKA Cream'.[7]

With Cream at Nation established, James Barton set about extending Cream's identity and activities beyond Merseyside. Cream's global reach grew to include nights at far-flung venues like Pacha in

Buenos Aires and an essential annual presence at Amnesia in Ibiza. In 1998 the Creamfields festival was launched and to date the event has been staged in fifteen different countries, from Mexico to Russia. Cream's transferability stems from the fact that its brand values of quality and purity are not Liverpool-specific and from the inherent potential for the re-assemblage of house music by DJs for its specific community in the moment at the location of consumption. James Barton capitalized on this raw potential to make Cream a worldwide phenomenon, but also the house-music flag bearer for Liverpool.

The date 12 October 2002 has gone down in Liverpool club scene history. It was Cream's tenth birthday party and the club's last regular Saturday at Nation. In the months and years leading up to this pivotal moment, Cream at Nation had gradually lost two generations of its audience. The house faithful who first renewed their community in the back room of the Academy had reacted against the growth and commercialization of the club. The new, fashionable crowd that Cream drew through the Rope Walks, together with the introduction of superstar DJs and slick branding, had served to alienate a significant portion of the club's original audience, who began to move on to newer club nights. Nevertheless, the weighing of its Liverpool anchor has had remarkably little effect on the Cream empire. As Cream at Nation came to an end, Creamfields was going from strength to strength, extending its global reach and holding onto its devoted UK audience of care-free outdoor clubbers. Cream Ibiza and a huge range of Cream residencies, tours and compilation albums are still doing good business. There was no resultant disconnect between the brand and the city either. Liverpool was still calling on the reputation and cachet of Cream to promote itself as a destination for cultural tourism during its year as European Capital of Culture, in 2008.[8] Cream remains the popular signifier for house music in Liverpool, despite the fact that what it signified to the Merseyside audience who conflated Nation and Cream into one unifying experience no longer exists.

Moving house

With each movement of the Liverpool house scene there has been an accompanying sense of loss. A sudden example of this occurred when Garlands, the house club on Eberle Street that is a cornerstone of a group of gay clubs and bars centred on Stanley Street, was set on fire in the summer of 2002. A candle-lit vigil was held outside during the blaze and over 300 hand-written messages of support were posted on the shell of the building in its aftermath. The Garlands community responded as if bereaved. Simon Reynolds had already dramatically announced a wider death of house in 1997: 'Rave culture – in so far as it has proved incapable of delivering on its utopian promise – has turned from living dream to living death' (Reynolds 1997: 84). But his proclamations are challenged by the tenacious ability of Liverpool's house scene to renew itself. The Garlands community stuck together. There was meaning beyond 'ever escalating exultation' and it was largely the love, peace, unity and positivity, which Reynolds is so quick to try to bury (Reynolds 1997: 84–86), that saw them through a temporary move to the State and a triumphant return to a rebuilt Eberle Street venue.

Successive waves of clubbers have certainly experienced loss and felt it keenly, whether it be first-generation ravers like Toni Mallon missing Larks in the Park, or Quadrant Park regulars needing to re-create their part of the Quad online, but those losses have provoked rebirths. Chibuku Shake Shake has been widely praised as a breath of fresh air for its house party feel, but also came out of a sense of something missing or lost. Damo Jones explains how it felt at the beginning:

> When Will [Jameson] and I started Chibuku, years and years ago, we had no idea what we were doing. It was for fun really. We were going out a lot in Liverpool and something seemed a bit off with it all, just a sense there was not much character in the clubs – apart from Bugged Out! which was always immense on a large scale. We had talked about an intimate club night for a while and then one Xmas, whilst we were both at our respective homes for the university break, we decided to go for it. Other than saying to give it a try, we had no idea what starting and promoting a club night actually entailed apart from the 'having fun' part.[9]

Chibuku's line-ups are eclectic, unexpectedly combining diverse post-rave genres in a way that challenges Reynolds' model of frag-mentation where, 'each post-rave fragment seems to have preserved one aspect of rave culture at the expense of the others' (Reynolds 1997: 85).

Reynolds' thesis is on safer ground when applied to Liverpool's own fragmented corner of rave: 'scouse house'. After years of importing house styles, Liverpool developed its own. Scouse house has a bouncy texture, characterized by rhythms of between 150 and 160 beats per minute, accentuated bass-lines on the second and fourth beat of every bar (which later became known as a 'donk'), mixed with elements such as staccato piano riffs, string arpeggios and speeded up happy hard-core-style vocal samples. In the 2000s scouse house developed as something of a self-enclosed scene in the city, with DJs such as Lee Butler, Les Calvert and Pez Tellet attracting large crowds to venues such as the (now closed) Ofiveone and the Buzz club. Despite the occasional foray in the national charts (such as 'Pretty Green Eyes', a 2003 hit for Mike Di Scala's Ultrabeat), scouse house existed, and continues to exist, beyond the realms of national fashion and media coverage. Indeed, while many of the original DJs associated with the term have moved on to other genres of electronic dance music, the scouse house scene continues to thrive. Live MCs work with DJs to deliver tracks in venues like the Pleasure Rooms on Wolstenholme Square and across the north-west of England. The lack of media exposure has meant that scouse house and its derivatives (such as bouncy or donk, which emerged as the style spread out to other areas of the north-west) constitute a genuinely underground movement which has spread through word of mouth, internet forums and social networking sites.

Like each moment in the history of Liverpool house music sketched in this brief and partial survey, scouse house highlights an aspect of the way in which the house scene interacts with the idea of place and the city of Liverpool. The genre is of Liverpool, but without traditional regional signifiers like accented vocal lines and place-referencing lyrics. As with other forms of house music, it becomes specific and local in the way that it is reassembled and enjoyed by its audience interacting with one another in the moment. The same fleeting magic experienced in a 'liminal' place has been captured, lost and sometimes recreated again by successive generations of Liverpool clubbers. Each time house music in Liverpool draws close to a traditional definition of place – fixed venues and re-generation zones – its audience pulls away. Yet the physicality of the city – its derelict buildings and its dislocated industrial estates – has influenced the trajectory of the house scene and left place markers in the memories of those who were there. These individual experiences coalesce into mutually reinforced collective identities and ultimately into a powerful and enduring sense of the house scene in Liverpool as particular, exceptional and very special.

Notes

1 For a summary of methodological approaches to academic research into dance scenes, see 'The Tribal Rites of Saturday Night: Discos and Intellectuals' in Gilbert and Pearson (1999).
2 'Rave' is a term first used in the 1980s to refer to acid house parties, which often took place in illegal or secret locations. The term has since become common within club culture to describe any dance music event which takes place outside the usual nightclub environment.
3 From the title of a 1995 house single by Josh Wink, 'Higher State of Consciousness'.
4 See also Wainwright (1990b).
5 'Left Side', posted on the forum www.quadrantpark.com ('the home of Quadrant Park nostalgia'), 2005 (accessed May 2009).
6 Toni Mallon quoted in *Tales from the Riverbank* (Domestic Films for Granada Television, 1999). It's likely that when talking about 'Groundbeat', Toni is referring to the Earthbeat events that took place in Sefton Park.
7 See www.outlar.com/listings.php?venue=nation (accessed June 2009).
8 For example Liverpool city council and the Liverpool Culture Company Limited put Cream alongside Merseybeat and the punk scene in the brochure *Sound City* (Liverpool, 2007).
9 Damo Jones, text for *The Beat Goes On* exhibition, 2008.

References

Du Noyer, Paul (2007) *Liverpool: Wondrous Place – Music from the Cavern to the Capital of Culture*. London: Virgin.
Fikentscher, Kai (2000) *'You Better Work!' Underground Dance Music in New York*. Middletown, CT: Wesleyan University Press.
Gilbert, Jeremy and Ewan Pearson (1999) *Discographies: Dance Music, Culture and the Politics of Sound*. London: Routledge.
Gilmore, Abigail (2004) 'Popular Music, Urban Regeneration and Cultural Quarters: The Case of the Rope Walks, Liverpool'. In: David Bell and Mark Jayne (eds) *City of Quarters: Urban Villages in the Contemporary City*. Aldershot: Ashgate. pp. 109–30.
Ingham, James (1999) 'Listening Back from Blackburn: Virtual Sound Worlds and the Creation of Temporary Autonomy'. In: Andrew Blake (ed.) *Living Through Pop*. London: Routledge. pp. 112–28.
Langlois, Tony (1992) 'Can You Feel It? DJs and House Music Culture in the UK'. *Popular Music* 11(2): 229–38.
Merseyside Socialist Research Group (1980) *Merseyside in Crisis*. Liverpool: Merseyside Socialist Research Group.

Reynolds, Simon (1997) 'Rave Culture: Living Dream or Living Death?' In: Steve Redhead (ed.) *The Clubcultures Reader.* Oxford: Blackwell. pp. 84–93.

Social and Spatial Inequalities Group (2008) *Changing City.* Sheffield: Social and Spatial Inequalities Group.

Spencer, Paul (ed.) (1985) *Society and the Dance.* Cambridge: Cambridge University Press.

Wainwright, Martin (1990a) '231 Arrested in Acid House Raid'. *Guardian,* 18 June. p. 20.

Wainwright, Martin (1990b) '800 Arrested in Acid House Raid'. *Guardian,* 23 July. p. 19.

Oral histories

James Barton, National Museums Liverpool, 26 March 2008.
Andy Carroll, National Museums Liverpool, 25 April 2008.
Mike Knowler, National Museums Liverpool, 22 April 2008.

CHAPTER 9

The creative process: Liverpool songwriters on songwriting

Marion Leonard

Introduction

Songwriters have been at the heart of Liverpool's reputation as a musical city. Indeed, the songwriting partnership forged by John Lennon and Paul McCartney did much to change wider perceptions about what a popular music artist stood for. Although they had immediate predecessors such as Chuck Berry and Buddy Holly, Lennon and McCartney's phenomenal success took the idea of the artist who both wrote and performed his or her own material to the centre of popular music practice. No longer was there a clear division of labour between the back-room craftsperson of the songwriter and the marketable star that characterized popular music practice from the Tin Pan Alley era onwards. Rather, the singer-songwriter became a singular unit of production, a configuration which became the norm of the rock era. This pragmatic shift within rock culture served further to change the relationship between audience and performer. The intimate connection between performer and material meant that songs became regarded as expressive of the performer's own thoughts, emotions and feelings.

Given this shift, it is perhaps unsurprising that there is a mystique around singer-songwriters, reinforced by film biopics, documentaries and the music press, which associates these musicians with emotional honesty, authenticity and artistic autonomy. Singer-songwriters have come to be seen as somewhat apart from or unpolluted by the pressures of a commercial industry, as independent artists who are able to express emotional insights and observations through song. The very process of songwriting has been mythologized, frequently characterized as either the dazzling brilliance of creative inspiration or the unique craft of the talented, creative individual.

Drawing on oral histories with Liverpool singer-songwriters, this chapter explores how they characterize the nature of their work. It considers how they describe the process of songwriting and the creative moment in which ideas are developed. Moreover, it discusses how the musicians reflect on the importance of place to the development of their music making. How has their experience of living and working in Liverpool influenced their songwriting and what are the pressures of being a songwriter in a city which is remembered as the birthplace of the most successful popular music group of all time?

The creative artist

Musicians and songwriters are often popularly understood and publicly constructed in ways which draw upon the romantic mythology of the creative artist. This represents creative individuals as possessing a natural and exceptional talent which marks them out from the ordinary, 'a set of powers peculiar to them that are beyond the grasp of mere mortals' (McIntyre 2008: 40). Such a mode of representing musicians can be seen most frequently within biographies and music journalism, where the creative individual is often described in mystical terms and portrayed as out of step with everyday life due to extraordinary talent. Liverpool musicians are no exception, as there is a long line of songwriters from the city who have been represented in this way. A prominent example can be seen in the way in which Lee Mavers, front person of the influential and critically acclaimed band the La's, has been described within press reports as an almost mythical figure. One *Guardian* review stated definitively that 'The word genius is often abused but it definitely applies to Lee Mavers' (Simpson 1998), while a review in the *Observer* portrayed him as burdened by his creativity and compared him to

Syd Barrett of Pink Floyd and Brian Wilson of the Beach Boys as other famed 'genius outsiders' from the music world:

> And in lead singer and main songwriter Lee Mavers, the group discovered a Syd Barrett figure for the Nineties – a forlorn and obsessive perfectionist with an eye for detail that single-handedly saw the group implode without a follow-up.... Had the group continued, The La's might have taken their rightful place alongside The Stone Roses and Primal Scream as cornerstones of British pop music. Only, Mavers – like Brian Wilson before him – seemed hellbent on articulating every sound in his head, tragically forfeiting his genius in the process. (Wazir 2000)

While these types of representation pervade the discourses which surround popular music, it is important not to take them completely at face value. For example, we should recognize that creativity takes place within an industrial context and it is clear that the music and media industries have an investment in perpetuating a mythology around musicians. As Jon Stratton (1983) has argued, it serves the interests of the music industry to present artists as exceptional, uniquely talented individuals spiritually cut off from the work-a-day realities, financial decision making and image manipulation of the music business. In making this observation I do not wish to downplay the nature of creative work but rather to recognize that creative artists have regularly been presented in ways which mark them out from the ordinary and erase the commercial and industrial frameworks which undoubtedly exert an influence upon the creative process. Indeed, as Keith Negus (1995: 329) has commented, creative production is often described in mystical ways which avert attention from 'the way in which pop is produced in a very conscious manner to meet deadlines, fit specific formats and to suit other day-to-day necessities involved in the industrial production of music'.

While these pragmatic and industrial factors are clearly important, we should perhaps be unsurprised by the tendency for romantic discourse to dominate, given the slipperiness of the notion of creativity itself. There is something intangible about the creative process which perhaps lends itself to romantic, mythologized readings of the singer-songwriter and there is often a difficulty in articulating exactly what goes on within moments of creativity. While creative artists have historically been constructed and mythologized in particular ways, the moment of creativity has often been described as something which is beyond their control. The impulse of creativity is often represented (both by artists themselves and by commentators) as mysterious, even magical – a pulse of creativity which travels through the individual. This understanding of artists represents them as a conduit, people through whom creativity flows, uninterrupted by rational, conscious thought. Paul Zollo refers to this idea of creative inspiration in the introduction to his book which collects together interviews with over fifty well known North American songwriters. Zollo comments that many of his interviewees said that:

> their greatest songs were written in a flash, words and music arriving simultaneously, like uncovering something that was already there. Even those who scoffed at the suggestion of a spiritual source of songs admitted that the process is mysterious and can't be controlled. (Zollo 1997: xii)

As with Zollo's respondents, a number of Liverpool musicians described the process of songwriting as mysterious, in that ideas for songs came to them seemingly unbidden. However, by describing the creative moment in this way, the musicians were not seeking to elevate their own status but were rather attempting to articulate the seemingly unconscious immediacy of creative ideas. For instance, in the following quotes John Head, of the Pale Fountains, the Strands and Shack, and singer-songwriter Kathryn Williams describe how sometimes songs just seem to come of their own volition:

> JOHN HEAD: I try not to think about it; it is one of them things that just sort of happens really ... situations just happen or something pops into your head and things like that. There is not really any situation where I have sat down and gone, 'Right, I have got to write three songs by six o'clock' or anything like that. It is just the sort of progression ... there are not many days go by where you are not picking your guitar up and if you do you play it the next day because you have missed it, sort of thing. I know that sounds really horrible but it's one of them things. Things happen and you are learning things yourself and you play and you go, 'Oh, that is interesting', and sometimes you just sit down and something just pours out of you quite simply and you ... really don't have that much to do with it. It is never the same really. It is not really an approach: it just happens to be honest.

> KATHRYN WILLIAMS: Some songs take a couple of years and other songs can be five minutes. I wrote 'Flicker' that is on the second record [*Little Black Numbers*, which was nominated for the Mercury

Prize] and I was working in a café and the words, the melody, the cello line, everything, just came on in my head as if someone had switched a radio on. It was like, I mean it is a complete gift and no effort on my behalf at all except to like pretend that I was going to the toilet with a pen and write the whole thing on loo roll and sing it all day, all day, all day, until I got home and pressed my tape player on and recorded it, you know. So that was more like capturing and when songs come to me like that I feel a bit of a fraud because I don't know where they have come from and I am just sort of like trying to catch it as much as I can and, yeah, it is a gift. And they are always the best ones.... You can really craft a song and chisel away like a sculpture until you have got the form right but the best ones are when they just come to you like that.

These comments express how ideas can come as impulses which are seemingly not consciously worked through in the ways that other ideas or practices might be. Some musicians highlighted the difficulty in describing the creative moment and turned to metaphors as a way to express how the creative process came about. For example, John Power, solo artist and former member of Cast and the La's, used the metaphor of fishing to describe the process of working out or developing an idea for a song. He also likened the practice of songwriting to tuning in a radio, referring to the random discovery that might come about when listening to broadcasts:

It comes down to just having the time, stroking the guitar, fishing for something. You just pull in a shape. You very rarely write a song you know beginning to end, lyrics finished, melody sorted; obviously you can get a block or something and it is going to change and meander its way through but no, it is just more ... you go 'Let's see what is on the airwaves today', like, you know.

Both Kathryn Williams and John Power used the metaphor of a radio to help to communicate the moment or sense that they have of how ideas come to them. For Williams, the metaphor was a way to describe the moment when a song comes to the fore of her consciousness 'as if someone had switched a radio on', while Power's description alludes to the chance encounter or fleeting nature of creative development as the artist grasps at ideas which are not at once fully formed but which 'meander' as he or she tunes across the 'airwaves'.

Influences and inspiration

As these descriptions of songwriting indicate, the way in which an idea for a song arrives can certainly feel mysterious or magical. Indeed, the musicians articulate how sometimes they have the sense that the idea has just been delivered fully formed, without conscious thought. So how then might this flash of inspiration be understood? The fact that this process can feel mysterious helps to explain why it is often mystified, accounted for as 'pure inspiration'. However, as numerous scholars have pointed out (Finnegan 1989; Toynbee 2000; Sawyer 2006; McIntyre 2008), a focus on the individual as the locus and originator of creative ideas does not recognize the conditions needed for creativity to arise or indeed how creative production, such as songwriting, typically involves a working knowledge of the creative work of others and can also involve collaboration with others in the process of creating something new.

Popular musicians develop their techniques, skills and practice through listening to others (Bennett 1980; Green 2002; Sawyer 2006). Over time, a musician builds up a store of knowledge about song structures, styles, genre conventions and techniques, and becomes familiar with different modes of songwriting which create different moods or offer different styles of articulation. With respect to this, drawing on the work of Bourdieu, Jason Toynbee (2000) has offered a very helpful way of thinking about songwriting. He puts forward the idea not of a self-sufficient, creative individual but of 'social authorship'. By this he means that songwriters, when working on a new idea, draw from their experiences of the past, including formative music lessons and their knowledge of performances which they have built up through listening and watching others. So, while songwriters do innovate and create new works, they are also drawing, albeit sometimes unconsciously, from their stores of knowledge about music. While this does not fully explain how new ideas are arrived at, it does help us to understand how the musician works with existing ideas, sound textures, lyrical conventions and song structures when developing, consciously or unconsciously, new ideas. The comments of Ian McNabb, solo artist and founder of the Icicle Works, can be taken as illustrative of this process, as he explains how frequently another piece of music acts as a stimulus, sparking off a creative idea:

A lot of the time what happens is I hear something on the radio or hear somebody else's song and think: 'Wow, I wish we would have written that'. So then I start trying to write something that is a bit like it and sometimes you can tell that you have taken the idea from somewhere but generally it is just a feeling you get. You go 'Wow, that is really such a great song and I love the way it does that', and you try and assimilate it and hopefully end up with something that has got somewhere close to it but isn't a direct rip off.

McNabb's comments highlight the balance which needs to be struck within songwriting between originality and the need to work within a convention or set of musical structures, often dictated by genre. So, the songwriter clearly has agency, but the creative work is produced with regard to knowledge of existing songs and techniques. As Phillip McIntyre notes, 'It is the task of the person, in this case a songwriter, to produce some variation in this inherited information, this set of conventions, rules, and ideas of what is, in effect, the structured knowledge of songs and songwriting that the individual songwriter has access to' (McIntyre 2008: 42). Kathryn Williams also commented on the necessity of working with and within particular writing conventions. She discussed how the topic of lost and found love is a recurrent theme within popular music and so the challenge of songwriting is to attend to this tradition while simultaneously making an original contribution:

Trying to say things that have been said loads of times without a cliché, I think that's the big thing. Because everyone loves, everyone wants to talk about love, and everyone wants to talk about lost love, and found love, but it is trying to say it in a way that ... makes it feel real but it is new, it is said in a new way for an old feeling.

While some musicians identified particular songs as sources of inspiration, others discussed how the style or performance of another musician had a strong influence upon them. Blues musician Connie Lush, for instance, made the following comment when discussing the development of her style:

I just follow what I like because I still love some of the stuff I used to do in the very beginning. I still like it and some of it is very embarrassing of course and you go 'Oh no!', but you just develop your style or you suddenly stumble upon someone who inspires you and you just run off and want to do that.

These comments perhaps point to the dominant way in which musicians learn about musical conventions, techniques and performance styles: that is, through listening to and watching other practitioners. This allows musicians to see 'what works' in terms of performance by watching stage presentation and audience reaction. Other musicians can also be important in demonstrating what is possible and in making the idea of being a musician seem like an achievable goal. John Head discussed this point by describing a memory which he has of watching an appearance of the Liverpool band the Teardrop Explodes on television with his brother Mick:

> Mick fell into it by accident and we just watched Teardrops on TV the night before on the Tony Wilson programme and … it was a local band and it is just really great to hear people with music that turns you on as well and it was sort of like, wow, you discovered someone else is into the similar-type thing as you and it was on telly. It was great. It was a really great moment and the next day Mick bumped into one of the bands in town and just said 'Do you want to join a band?'… That was one of them things that even, although you learn an instrument, you don't really think that is achievable almost.

The craft of songwriting

In contrast to their descriptions of songs which seemed to come spontaneously, local musicians also discussed how many songs were developed over time. Rather than the model of channelling or witnessing outlined above, here songwriting was described much more in terms of craft, whereby songs were worked at and honed through experimentation and refinement. This is a different under-standing of the process of songwriting than that of the 'genius' inspiration model but, of course, is still about the development and testing out of creative ideas. Ian Broudie, producer, solo artist and founder of the Lightning Seeds, commented on how he routinely experiments with ideas until he arrives at a sound and structure he feels is right:

> I always write melodies and then I set everything; everything comes around the melody. I'll find the chords and I'll find the words, I'll find the mood and, you know, try it a lot of different ways. I'm not someone who just sits down. I'll just, I'll have a tune really quickly

but I'll probably try it loads of different ways before I find out how it should be.

Similarly, Kathryn Williams discussed how some of her ideas for songs would develop over a long period. To enable this she habitually documents ideas and observations which she can then draw upon at a later date:

> Sometimes I will sit and play my guitar and chords will come and a melody will come in my head; other times, I mean, I have a notebook with me all the time and if something makes me want to write in that notebook I write in it and it might be a sentence that turns into a song a year later but I write all the time.

Her comments reveal that in some instances a song might develop from an initial idea expressed through a single line:

> I like thinking of ... really small things and really big things and, like, seeing an old couple ... hold hands to cross a road will inspire me to think about ... what life is about or the stillness of the day and, you know, the smell of a room will make me think of being a child again and just constantly sort of working out what it's about and what life's about and what love is about.

Mike Jones (2005: 238) has remarked on this mode of observational songwriting and noted that the process of song development can often begin with phrases collected 'from the discursive flux of everyday life' such as 'dialogue in films, television programmes, conversations overheard in public spaces'. Williams' practice of keeping a notebook demonstrates a discipline in the recording of ideas as they occur but also highlights the unpredictable way in which creative ideas surface. She could not predict when an idea might arise; often these might be everyday observations or reflections which can then be used within a song and so a notebook was necessary to record or capture germs of ideas, which could be worked on or transformed into a song at a later date. In this instance, while the craft of songwriting lies in developing and working through an idea, the conditions which enable a creative idea to form could not always or easily be manufactured. Williams' comments illustrate how moments of inspiration are necessarily situated within a wider creative consciousness, whereby the creative individual is constantly open to ideas. Part of the songwriting process, therefore, is in the collection, collation and editing of everyday experience, where observations are recorded, adapted and given significance. Indeed, a tacit recognition of what will work within a given structural context is a key element in understanding inspiration and creativity.

Structure and process

Thus, the way in which a song is brought into being involves moving from an original idea into a structured composition by the process of creative endeavour. As Ian Broudie commented, this process of realization can be frustrating, as an idea for a song might not always be translated, or even translatable, into a final recorded work:

> Probably for me the best bit really is when you've written something and it sounds great, because recording it is always a different task; playing it live is a different task but when you've just written it in your head I think that's when it sounds perfect, you know, and it never ever sounds like that again.

Part of the mystique of songwriting is precisely this process of translation from an initial phrase or idea into a fully realized musical composition. While songwriters approach this process in distinct ways, clearly an underlying knowledge of song structures and conventions is crucial. As the extensive ethnographic research conducted by McIntyre (2008: 46–47) has shown, songwriters draw on their knowledge of the 'domain of songwriting', which includes an understanding of 'the formal structure, conceptual schema, or set of generative conventions that organize the experience of music into song'. John Head's comments refer to this practice as he discusses how he brings a song together by fixing his initial ideas into a framework:

> It is never the same, it really isn't. Sometimes you will get a group of words in your head and other times ... generally, I actually have the music and quite soon I will develop it into a song. I will put the lyrics, the lyrics come part and parcel with it, and it will be a matter of actually developing it into a structure ... because the initial idea can be quite narrow so you have got to widen it and make it ... make sense.

Knowledge of these song structures is often so well embedded that songwriters may not consciously acknowledge that they are drawing from a bank of experience established through years of listening and performance. While making reference to the importance of establishing the basic structure of a song, John Head also represented the process as one of good fortune and luck rather than one based upon technical skill and artistic judgement:

> To actually find the bones of a song and then turn it into a piece of music and words that go together, that you are happy with, is a little bit like winning the lottery.... If you are really happy with it there is not much that is better than that.

Learning the trade

Just as individual songs are often shaped and developed over time, so also it is important to recognize that the skill of songwriting does not come *ex nihilo* but is a practice which is gradually learned, a set of skills to be honed. The journey of 'becoming' a musician usually takes a number of routes. In some cases skill development involves formal training, with instrumental tutors or instruction at school. As John Head recalls:

> I started music in school ... me and a gang of kids got together, because we have had a cupboard full of musical instruments that never got touched so we decided 'let's make this happen' and we had a really good teacher who showed us the right way to go about it and we got it.... We just used to have a lesson every Wednesday ... just us sitting, playing guitars in the classroom, so it was really cool.... It was better than maths.

Often, particularly in the case of popular music, the development of playing skills involves informal learning and *ad hoc* tuition from friends and family. Music techniques and styles of playing are often picked up from family members or through friendship groups, who might also provide the motivation to become a performer. Other social institutions, such as the church, can also provide an early introduction to music performance. As Joe Ankrah of the Chants remembers, church services were very significant in the development of his musical tastes and the establishment of his future musical direction:

> [My dad was] the organist and choir master of a church called the African Churches Mission, Upper Hill Street in Liverpool.... One of the most beautiful things about going to church was the way they used to sing hymns and the harmonies.... When you heard those deep rich voices singing harmonies and stuff like that, you know, it was absolutely brilliant, absolutely fantastic.

Other musicians commented that they had developed skills from following self-tuition books. Bill Drummond, for example, bought a copy of Burt Weedon's book *Play in a Day*. First published in 1957, this guitar tutor book proved so popular that it has sold over two million copies. Similarly, John Head commented that he had learned from a book of Beatles songs: 'you would know all the songs and it was a really useful way of learning how you had to do it right and where you were going wrong really as well'. While learning how to play classical music is usually undertaken through formal instruction, self-tuition is much more typical within the practice of popular music. Ian Broudie and Kathryn Williams both commented that they had adopted an auto-didactic approach which allowed them to try out ideas privately, learning through experimentation and mistakes.

> IAN BROUDIE: I don't remember not playing the guitar, if you know what I mean ... I taught myself ... I always played the guitar ... you know, not that well, but since I was really little and I was always obsessed with music so it never really felt like I was going to do anything else really.

> KATHRYN WILLIAMS: I didn't do any qualification for music. I was doing an art degree up in Newcastle and I had a guitar and I would secretly play it in my bedroom.... I'd put my fingers somewhere on the guitar and I'd think 'Oh, I've invented a chord' and then someone would tell me it was a D or something.

There are, of course, a host of ways in which musicians can develop skills, including tips in magazines and tuition videos posted on YouTube. However, the findings of a study by Lucy Green were that 'the overriding leaning practice for the beginner ... is to copy recordings by ear' (Green 2002: 60). This type of learning usually takes place 'outside of any formal networks, usually at early stages of learning, in isolation from each other, [and] without adult guidance' (Green 2002: 61). Others have also noted the prevalence of this practice, which allows beginners to develop their playing at their own pace (Bennett 1980; Finnegan 1989). Green found that, although this is common, musicians often did not recognize it as learning at all, but frequently dismissed it as something they did privately and which wasn't worth remarking on. Nevertheless, this practice of listening and copying is an important way in which skills are developed and through which musicians learn about song structures and composition. Garry Christian, solo artist and lead singer for the Christians, commented on how important listening to the records owned by his father and siblings was for the development of his vocal technique:

> The gramophone ... was in the front parlour and no one went in the front parlour because it was like the good room, you know, the tiny room, the clean room. We had a big family so that door was always locked, you know, but I knew where the key was so I used to whizz in there and take the records.... I used to go in and listen to all the records there and just listen to the voices of the likes of Ray Charles and the early Temptations and the Motown stuff. It was like incredible for me ... I would try and mimic them and try and learn.

Ian McNabb similarly commented that listening to and copying from recordings was a method which allowed him to develop his musical skills. While he went on to have formal classical guitar training, and also honed his skills through practising with others, copying recordings was his way into becoming a professional musician:

> When I saw Marc Bolan on *Top of the Pops* he had one of those Gibson flying Vs that is shaped like a V, like an arrow and I just thought, 'What is that all about?', you know. And then managed to borrow one off somebody which had [a high] action on it like that which was impossible to play. But the great thing about T. Rex records was that he couldn't really play either, so all the songs were dead easy to play, an E or A or G or C, very easy chords and a great way to start really because the Beatles chords were all sort of complicated and jazzy. So, yeah, with Marc Bolan songs you could just learn three chords and bash them and it nearly sounded like the record you know, du, dun, dun, dun, dun, dun or do, do, do, do type stuff.

Songwriting as participatory

The perpetuation of the romantic ideology of the creative artist within popular music discourse helps to reinforce the idea that songwriting is generally a solo endeavour. The legal protection of copyright further cements the idea that song development originates from one individual, as it grants rights, associated with a creative work, to a named creator. Yet, as Sawyer (2006: 226) argues, 'The member of the band who is credited as the writer of the song typically does no more than suggest the melodic line for the voice, the overall chord structure of the song, and the general style or genre of the piece'. Rather than being conceived of as complete works, songs are frequently arrived at through 'jamming' or working out ideas for melodies and riffs between musicians. Connie Lush, for example, discussed how she might generate the initial idea for a song which would then be developed by working with other members of her band:

> For me the beat is very, very important, the rhythm, and once I get the rhythm that I am after, the genre of the song, just to put it simply, if I want it slow, fast, funky, whatever, and then I am off and then I will start singing it until I have got what I want and I sing forever. And then I get the guys together and just say the style I want: if I want them to play slide, if I want it really bluesy, if I want it a bit more contemporary blues. It is all thrown out there you know and then it develops.

This comment offers a way of understanding creativity 'as a cultural process rather than a heroic act' (Toynbee 2003: 110). Each musician contributes elements or ideas for a song but the final arrangement is worked out through collaboration and experimentation. Similarly, Eddie Amoo of the Real Thing emphasized that collaboration was part of his regular mode of composition:

> The way we go about composing has never changed.... I'll have an idea; it usually starts off on my guitar, whereas I'm playing some chords on the guitar and I think that sounds good and I'll think of ... a nice melody to go over it, you know, start hearing these riffs in my head and Christopher will basically do the same. But whereas I usually start off on guitar, Christopher will start off on bass and then the two things come together and we sort of, like, meld them together.... That's how we've always worked and we still work like that now.

The ways in which creative work is undertaken are also shaped by the genres within which musicians work. While rock, soul or blues musicians might develop a song through jamming with other musicians, artists working within hip-hop or electronica might develop tracks through other sorts of collaboration. This is not to ignore artists who work alone – indeed, it should be acknowledged that musicians working within electronica often compose and self-produce entire albums – but rather to consider how artists working within these genres may have different forms of collaborative practice. Hip-hop artist Kof, for example, described how he frequently works with producers on the development of a track. The foundation of such a track might be a beat or a rhythm, which he then develops by adding a melody line and lyrics. The following comment reveals that he does not follow a uniform or standard way of developing ideas, so while songs might be composed in the studio from a mood or vibe, other ideas might develop out of observations of everyday life:

> There's a lot of different ways [to write tracks] … like I get a lot of music sent to me. A lot of producers get in touch and say 'Okay would you like to rap on this beat or sing on such and such?' So, there's that way and I listen to the music … what the vibe is. It could be, like, maybe a summer type of vibe and that makes me want to write … so it's all about what the music makes me feel and makes me think, just from hearing it, and I write from that. But there's other things that may happen socially round Liverpool on the news, when I'm walking to the studio, just a bunch of different things what I might see and think, 'You know what, that might be something that I haven't heard anybody talk about before, let me go and write about that'.

Place and music traditions

As Strachan has discussed in chapter 3 – as have other critics (Du Noyer 2007) – local musicians have often drawn inspiration from their experience of Liverpool. This can be evidenced by the considerable number of songs reflecting on the character of the city and mentioning particular locations. While there is not space here to offer a full list of songs which reference the city, one can consider 'Heart as Big as Liverpool' by the Mighty Wah!, Amsterdam's 'Does This Train Stop on Merseyside?', 'Liverpool Girl' by Ian McNabb and the passionate critique of city rebranding by Jegsy Dodd and the Original Sinners 'Liverpool 2008'. Some of these songs are celebrations or sentimental portraits of Liverpool but other evocations of place have been responses to the darker side of city living. Shack's portrait of heroin addiction in 'Streets of Kenny' can be taken as an illustration, in that it documents the gritty side of urban life in the Liverpool district of Kensington. Similarly Kof, working within the genre conventions of hip-hop, commented that his work often draws on his observations of the challenges of urban life and instances of social injustice. He discusses how the brutal, racially motivated murder of Anthony Walker in Huyton in 2005 was something on which he felt compelled to comment within his work:

> Obviously the stuff that happened with Anthony Walker – that was definitely something that I felt I needed to speak about, being a young black man in Liverpool. Because, obviously, it's not just me but a lot of people have been affected by racism in the city so I think it was good to talk on their behalf and on my behalf.

The ways in which the musicians articulated their relationship to place differed markedly, highlighting the multiple ways in which environment can affect creativity and expression. John Power, for instance, discussed how the city figured in his boyhood imagination as a place of prestige and achievement:

> What Liverpool gave me was an attitude. You know, I don't think I would have been the same if I was from Bolton ... there was a certain something ... 'Hey dad, who is the best band in the world?' ... 'The Beatles'. 'Where are they from?' 'They are from Liverpool'. I am from Liverpool. And this is like a four-year-old, a five-year-old or something like that you know. 'Who is the best footie team?' ... 'Liverpool are, you know'. Shankley. Liverpool. All of a sudden Liverpool was just here. I can remember being absolutely, deeply upset when I found out Liverpool wasn't the capital of anything ... we weren't even the biggest city. I can remember now, I must have been about nine, playing footie, you know, in school games and someone went: 'Oh Birmingham is bigger than Liverpool' and I was going 'It isn't you know' and then I realized it is just a city.

Power's mention of the Beatles highlights the significant place they have within the cultural imagination of the city. As other contributors to this book have observed (Leigh in chapter 2, Strachan in chapter 3), the Beatles are part of how the city is imagined, constructed, marketed and inhabited. Although the interviews discussed here can be taken only as personal responses, they are revealing of the different ways in which musicians navigate and draw from Liverpool's music heritage. In discussions of their creative practice, many musicians commented on how the Beatles had inspired them. Garry Christian, for example, commented that they were 'a huge influence on me and not just me but a lot of musicians in Liverpool and if anyone says they didn't they are lying as far as I am concerned'. Ian Broudie went further, pointing out that while the Beatles may have had a local influence, their impact was global: 'people often ask, you know, "You're from Liverpool. Have the Beatles influenced you?" and you think, well, if you're living on planet Earth the Beatles will influence you.' Musicians described this influence as operating in a number of ways. Eddie Amoo, for instance, recounted how listening to the band had provided a stimulus for his own songwriting:

> In the very beginning I used to ... write ... love songs and stuff and then when I heard a song by the Beatles called 'Eleanor Rigby' ... I was so fascinated by the song because I realized this was a song about life itself.... Basically I realized that you could sit down and you could write serious songs that really meant something about real life, what was really going on.... That took me into sort of, like, writing about stuff that was going on round me and stuff that I was actually experiencing while I was growing up.

For some, the Beatles were empowering as examples of what is possible. They acted as role models, encouraging others to pursue their own music ambitions. As John Head remarked:

> Liverpool is a place where ... one of the biggest bands in the world come from and that gives you the knowledge that you can actually achieve anything in music.... The Beatles kicked [down] the door and started writing their own music. There was other artists, obviously, doing that but there wasn't many in their position and I think that has given youngsters the confidence to go, you know: What is wrong with my song? Why not? Have a go.

Sara Cohen's ethnographic research with local rock musicians found that many 'acknowledge their debt to the Beatles and to local history and heritage, but the Beatles are also felt to be a constraining factor on their music, image and career' (Cohen 1997: 99). For some, the success of this band has tended to overshadow rather than facilitate ongoing music scenes. While many musicians currently working in the city may no longer feel this so keenly, the way in which the Beatles have created a certain image for the city is still seen by some as problematic. The Beatles and the success of subsequent rock bands have perhaps established an understanding of Liverpool as having a particular music tradition. While this might assist up-and-coming songwriters and guitar-based bands in attracting the attention of artists and repertoire (A&R) personnel, artists working in other music genres may not always welcome this association. Kof, for instance, commented:

> I don't relate to them [the Beatles] – they're not of my time ... although ... it's good music to listen to, it has never influenced the music that I make ... stop going on about the Beatles, like, look at the new talent ... obviously there's a few different groups and stuff, but what they're doing now is based on the door that the Beatles opened and that's why they've got so many outlets to be able to do their thing because everyone thinks 'Well, we had the Beatles: they were massive, loads of bands are going to come through' ... and other bands have come through ... but I think we need that for the urban scene so the urban scene can do that ... everyone knows Liverpool now, the Capital of Culture and the Beatles ... I'm trying to show them other different parts of Liverpool what might be going on.

Indeed, as Jayne Casey, formerly of Big in Japan, Pink Military and Pink Industry, argued, while the Beatles have put Liverpool on the musical map, it is subsequent commercially successful artists and creative music scenes which have maintained the city's reputation as a centre for music production:

> Each time there is a music scene it could just be a one-off. It has to be followed by something else that has world dominance. So, you know, if the Beatles had just come from Liverpool it would have meant not that much by now. So, the Bee Gees are from Manchester, so what? It was the fact that Eric's followed it and then Cream follows and so it starts to build up, this thing.

Clearly the reputation of Liverpool as a music city is important to musicians working within it, not least because this encourages an ongoing culture of music production. The following comments from Ian Broudie and Ian McNabb offer a very situated sense of creative production, where the surrounding conditions – availability of music, local tastes, social relationships, modes of sociality and cultural values – affect and influence creative practice. In this sense, creative work is sponsored and nurtured through the social context of its production.

IAN BROUDIE: What I would say is that Liverpool is a musical town. I think when you go out in Liverpool you hear a wide variety of music. A lot of the time in London you'll just hear what's the current trend.... Certainly, growing up in Liverpool, you hear country and western, punk ... I think you can be in a certain place and there'll be all different types of people who are into different music so you get a big cross-section of things. Plus, when I was growing up, Liverpool was quite a depressed place, you know, well, certainly when I was in my teens and I think ... everyone I knew was passionate about music and that might have just been the people I knew but it felt like everyone was passionate about music.

IAN McNABB: [I'm] very proud of the musical heritage that Liverpool has always had and still seems to have. You know, if you go out and see a band or you go out for a pint there is always a bunch of kids there who [have] just started a band, who just love *Forever Changes* or *Revolver* and their enthusiasm is pretty infectious and everyone just seems to be in a band and everybody wants to try and better each other.... There is always this thing of 'Oh, I heard your new single and it's brilliant' or 'I have been in the praccy all day and you want to hear this tune – like "Tomorrow Never Knows" but better'.... I don't know if you would get that in Hull.

Conclusion

These differing ways in which individual musicians position themselves in relation to the city's musical heritage are indicative of the way in which we can understand the creative process as a social process. Songwriting is bound up with a variety of social contexts which have an active effect upon creative practice. Elements such as place, genre and musical education affect the way in which songwriters approach their work and their relative positions to these elements become manifest in differing ways. An acknowledgement of songwriting as a social process does not, however, simply reduce creativity to a mundane pragmatism. After all, not all of us have the capacity to move listeners through our creative endeavours, even if we have spent years trying. Successful songwriters are clearly creative people who have agency within their own practice and are highly adept at channelling this creativity into artistic works which have an emotional resonance among audiences. Indeed, this chapter has described how they internalize nuanced elements of songwriting standards and performance conventions in the creation of new and meaningful work. It has also outlined how songwriters are attuned to the creative possibilities of routine experience through a creative consciousness whereby snippets of everyday speech and occurrence, emotion and feeling provide the basis for inspiration.

This is highly significant, as songwriting is a form which is ultimately bound up with the communication of experience, a function which Negus and Pickering (2004) see as central to the concept of creativity. For a songwriter to have the power to move, surprise and inspire listeners, this function is necessarily combined with a developed sense of imagination and inventiveness. In Negus and Pickering's terms, this is what marks out certain creative artists and artistic works with a sense of 'exceptionality'. Certain individuals are both highly skilled at manipulating the musical codes and structures that constitute the 'craft' of songwriting and possess a developed imaginative capacity. Thus, for Negus and Pickering (2004: 154) 'the painstakingly acquired creative know-how of the painter, musician or writer is drawn on to harness the stream of mental play and fantasy to certain devices and conventions while retaining the spirit of inventiveness'. This chapter has sought to examine these differing elements of creativity by taking into account the first-hand accounts of Liverpool songwriters in order to reveal how these factors combine within their own practice. The way that their voices are shot through with a mixture of pragmatism, imagination and metaphor is perhaps a fitting articulation of the creative process itself.

References

Bennett, H. Sith (1980) *On Becoming a Rock Musician*. Amherst, MA: University of Massachusetts Press.

Cohen, Sara (1997) 'Liverpool and the Beatles: Exploring Relations Between Music and Place, Text and Context'. In: David Schwarz, Anahid Kassabian and Lawrence Siegel (eds) *Keeping Score: Music, Disciplinarity, Culture*. Charlottesville, VA: University Press of Virginia. pp. 90–106.

Du Noyer, Paul (2007) 'Subversive Dreamers: Liverpool Songwriting from the Beatles to the Zutons'. In: Rees-Deryn Jones and Michael Murphy (eds) *Writing Liverpool: Essays and Interviews*. Liverpool: Liverpool University Press. pp. 239–51.

Finnegan, Ruth (1989) *The Hidden Musicians: Music-Making in an English Town*. Cambridge: Cambridge University Press.

Green, Lucy (2002) *How Popular Musicians Learn: A Way Ahead for Music Education*. Aldershot: Ashgate.

Jones, Mike (2005) 'Writing for Your Supper: Creative Work and the Contexts of Popular Songwriting'. In: John Williamson (ed.) *Words and Music: Liverpool Music Symposium 3*. Liverpool: Liverpool University Press. pp. 219–49.

McIntyre, Phillip (2008) 'Creativity and Cultural Production: A Study of Contemporary Western Popular Music Songwriting'. *Creativity Research Journal* 20(1): 40–52.

Negus, Keith (1995) 'Where the Mystical Meets the Market: Creativity and Commerce in the Production of Popular Music'. *Sociological Review* 43(2): 316–41.

Negus, Keith and Michael Pickering (2004) *Creativity, Communication and Cultural Value*. London: Sage.

Sawyer, R. Keith (2006) *Explaining Creativity: The Science of Human Innovation*. Cary, NC: Oxford University Press

Simpson, Dave (1998) 'The Lost Boy'. *Guardian*, 5 December. p. 4.

Stratton, Jon (1983) 'Capitalism and Romantic Ideology in the Record Business'. *Popular Music* 3: 143–56.

Toynbee, Jason (2000) *Making Popular Music: Musicians, Creativity and Institutions*. London: Arnold.

Toynbee, Jason (2003) 'Music, Culture, and Creativity'. In: Martin Clayton, Trevor Herbert and Richard Middleton (eds) *The Cultural Study of Music: A Critical Introduction*. London: Routledge. pp. 102–12.

Wazir, Burhan (2000) 'There They Go Again: The La's, The La's'. *Observer*, 24 December. p. 15.

Zollo, Paul (1997) *Songwriters on Songwriting*. New York: Da Capo Press.

Oral histories

Eddie Amoo, National Museums Liverpool, 29 April 2008.

Joe Ankrah, National Museums Liverpool, 4 June 2008.

Ian Broudie, National Museums Liverpool, 24 April 2008.

Jayne Casey, National Museums Liverpool, 27 February 2009.

Garry Christian, National Museums Liverpool, 4 June 2008.

Bill Drummond, National Museums Liverpool, 12 May 2008.

John Head, National Museums Liverpool, 4 June 2008.

Kof, National Museums Liverpool, 12 May 2008.

Connie Lush, National Museums Liverpool, 25 June 2008.

Ian McNabb, National Museums Liverpool, 27 May 2008.

John Power, National Museums Liverpool, 25 May 2008.

Kathryn Williams, National Museums Liverpool, 13 June 2008.

Index

Band in the Crowd 91–92
Bandits 58, 59
Bangs, Lester 23
Barbel 109
Barrett, Syd 163
Barton, James 146, 147–48, 149, 152–53, 155, 156
Bassett, Timmy 88
Bassey, Shirley 94
Beat City 53
Beatlemania 17, 31
Beatles 17, 43–44
  and Apple Corps 54–55
  and black musicians 85–86
  and Decca 13
  'Eleanor Rigby' 30
  heritage sites 80
  'In My Life' 37, 51, 62n
  innovation and change 37
  and Liverpool 3–4, 11, 21, 31–33, 37–41, 53, 54, 176
  look 36
  'Maggie Mae' 49, 50
  'Penny Lane' and 'Strawberry Fields' 37, 51–52
  re-evaluation 21–24
  and skiffle 13–14
  and songwriters 172, 176–78
  stagecraft 15–16
  and United States 17, 20, 35–36
Beatles Anthology 54–55
Beatles Rock Band 55
Beatles' Story, The 53
Bee Gees 36
Behan, Dominic 47, 49
Belcham, John 45, 49–50, 61, 62
Bennett, Andy 81
Best, Pete 15
Bexy Sitch and the Creepy Crawlies 109
Big Dig 65, 82n
Big in Japan 109, 118–19, 126, 127, 138, 139, 140
  Eric's 136
  formation 136–37
Big Three 14, 17

Birkenhead 72
Black 57
Black, Cilla 31, 48, 49, 108
black communities 86–88
black musicians 5–6, 84–85, 101–2, 103n
  and black America 89–92
  clubs 129
  music industry 93–98
  Real Thing and Brit-soul 98–101
'Blackbird' (McCartney) 37
Blackmailers 137
  see also Spitfire Boys
Blige, Mary J. 102
Blue Album (Beatles) 54
Blue Notes 108
Bolan, Marc 173
Bold Street 152–3
Bolland, Anthony 81
Bolland, Philip 50
Boone, Pat 12
Bootle 150–52
Boys from the Blackstuff 44
Bradley, Dick 23
Brenda and the Beachballs 109
Bright, Bette 109
Brit-soul 6, 98–101
Brocken, Michael 5, 47, 48
Broudie, Ian 109, 118, 126
  on Eagle 134
  Eric's 132, 135–36, 137–38
  Mathew Street 129
  songwriting 168–69, 170, 172, 177, 178, 179
Browne, Tommy 94
Budgie 119, 137
Buenos Aires 155–56
Bugged Out! 157
Burns, Pete 136, 137
Burns Owens Partnership 106
Burtonwood 89, 103n
Butcher, Mike 111
Butler, Lee 158
Button Street 125
Buzz 158
Buzz Brothers 90